The
Epicurus
Reader

The Epicurus Reader

Selected Writings and Testimonia

Translated and Edited,
with Notes, by
Brad Inwood
and
L. P. Gerson

Introduction by
D. S. Hutchinson

Hackett Publishing Company, Inc.
Indianapolis / Cambridge

Epicurus: 341 B.C.–271 B.C.

Copyright © 1994 by Hackett Publishing Company, Inc.
Printed in the United States of America

Cover design by Listenberger Design and Associates
Text design by Dan Kirklin

For further information, please address
  Hackett Publishing Company, Inc.
  P.O. Box 44937
  Indianapolis, Indiana 46244–0937

        10 09 08 07 06 05 04   4 5 6 7 8 9 10

Library of Congress Cataloging-in-Publication Data

Epicurus.
    [Works. English. 1994]
    The Epicurus reader: selected writings and testimonia translated
    and edited, with notes, by Brad Inwood and L. P. Gerson;
    introduction by D. S. Hutchinson.
        p.   cm.
    Includes bibliographical references and index.
    ISBN 0-87220-242-9   ISBN 0-87220-241-0 (pbk.)
    I. Inwood, Brad.   II. Gerson, Lloyd P.   III. Title.
    B570.E5I582   1994
    187—dc20   93-44073
                                                            CIP

Contents

The four-part cure

(Philodemus, Herculaneum Papyrus 1005, 4.9–14)

Don't fear god,
Don't worry about death;
What is good is easy to get, and
What is terrible is easy to endure.

Introduction

Do you want to be happy? Of course you do! Then what's standing in your way? Your happiness is entirely up to you. This has been revealed to us by a man of divine serenity and wisdom who spent his life among us, and showed us, by his personal example and by his teaching, the path to redemption from unhappiness. His name was Epicurus.

This is the sort of thing you might have heard an Epicurean preaching in the market square of an ancient city. If it sounds like a religious message, that is no coincidence; Epicurus was revered by his followers as though divine, a sage who had answers to all the important questions of life. What attracted converts was the prospect of personal happiness, for which Epicurus offered clear philosophical advice.

The fundamental obstacle to happiness, says Epicurus, is anxiety. No matter how rich or famous you are, you won't be happy if you're anxious to be richer or more famous. No matter how good your health is, you won't be happy if you're anxious about getting sick. You can't be happy in this life if you're worried about the next life. You can't be happy as a human being if you're worried about being punished or victimized by powerful divine beings. But you *can* be happy if you believe in the four basic truths of Epicureanism: there are no divine beings which threaten us; there is no next life; what we actually need is easy to get; what makes us suffer is easy to put up with. This is the so-called 'four-part cure', the Epicurean remedy for the epidemic sickness of human anxiety; as a later Epicurean puts it, "Don't fear god, don't worry about death; what's good is easy to get, and what's terrible is easy to endure."[1]

"What's good is easy to get." We need food, water, shelter from the elements, and safety from hostile animals and people. All these things lie ready to hand and can be acquired with little effort or money. We don't need caviar, champagne, palaces, or bodyguards, which are expensive and difficult to acquire and keep. People who want more than they need are making a fundamental mistake, a mistake that reduces their chances of being satisfied and causes needless anxiety. While our bodies need food, water, shelter, and safety, all that our souls need is to be confident that our bodies will get what they need. If my body is contented and my

1. Philodemus of Gadara, from a work whose title is uncertain, preserved in Herculaneum Papyrus 1005, column IV, lines 10–14.

soul is confident, then I will be cheerful, and being cheerful is the key to being happy. As long as we are cheerful it takes very little to keep us happy, but without cheerfulness we cannot really enjoy even the so-called 'pleasures' of life. Being cheerful is a state which is full of pleasure—indeed Epicurus calls it 'the limit of pleasure'—and it is a normal state, but if we suffer from anxiety we need to train ourselves to attain and maintain it. The discipline of Epicurean philosophy enables its followers to recognize how little they actually need, to enjoy possessing it, and to enjoy the confidence that they will continue to possess it. On the other hand, there is no reason not to enjoy occasional luxuries, if they happen to be easily available. There is nothing wrong with luxury in itself, but any dependence on luxuries is harmful to our happiness, as is every desire for unnecessary things.

"What's terrible is easy to endure." There is no denying that illness and pain are disagreeable, but nature has so constituted us that we need not suffer very much from them. Sickness is either brief or chronic, and either mild or intense, but discomfort that is both chronic and intense is very unusual; so there is no need to be concerned about the prospect of suffering. This is admittedly a difficult teaching to accept, especially for young people, but as people get older and more experienced in putting up with suffering, they tend to recognize its truth more and more, as did the Roman philosopher Seneca, whose health was anything but strong.[2] Epicurus himself died in excruciating pain, from kidney failure after two weeks of pain caused by kidney stones; but he died cheerfully, he claimed, because he kept in mind the memory of his friends and the agreeable experiences and conversations they had had together. Mental suffering, unlike physical suffering, is agony to endure, but once you grasp the Epicurean philosophy you won't need to face it again. Know the limits of what you need, recognize the limits of what your body is likely to suffer, and enjoy the confidence that your life will be overwhelmingly pleasant, unless you poison it with anxiety.

"Don't worry about death." While you are alive, you don't have to deal with being dead, but when you are dead you don't have to deal with it either, because you aren't there to deal with it. "Death is nothing to us," as Epicurus puts it, for "when we exist, death is not yet present, and when death is present, then we do not exist."[3] Death is always irrelevant to us, even though it causes considerable anxiety to many people for much of their lives. Worrying about death casts a general pall over the

---

2. Seneca, *Letters to Lucilius* lxxviii.7–10.

3. Epicurus, *Letter to Menoeceus* (text 4), section 125.

experience of living, either because people expect to exist after their deaths and are humbled and terrified into ingratiating themselves with the gods, who might well punish them for their misdeeds, or else because they are saddened and terrified by the prospect of *not* existing after their deaths. But there are no gods which threaten us, and, even if there were, we would not be there to be punished. Our souls are flimsy things which are dissipated when we die, and even if the stuff of which they were made were to survive intact, that would be nothing to us, because what matters to us is the continuity of our experience, which is severed by the parting of body and soul. It is not sensible to be afraid of ceasing to exist, since you already know what it is like not to exist; consider any time before your birth—was it disagreeable not to exist? And if there is nothing bad about not existing, then there is nothing bad for your friend when he ceases to exist, nor is there anything bad for you about being fated to cease to exist. It is a confusion to be worried by your mortality, and it is an ingratitude to resent the limitations of life, like some greedy dinner guest who expects an indefinite number of courses and refuses to leave the table.

"Don't fear god." The gods are happy and immortal, as the very concept of 'god' indicates. But in Epicurus' view, most people were in a state of confusion about the gods, believing them to be intensely concerned about what human beings were up to and exerting tremendous effort to favour their worshippers and punish their mortal enemies. No; it is incompatible with the concept of divinity to suppose that the gods exert themselves or that they have any concerns at all. The most accurate, as well as the most agreeable, conception of the gods is to think of them, as the Greeks often did, in a state of bliss, unconcerned about anything, without needs, invulnerable to any harm, and generally living an enviable life. So conceived, they are role models for Epicureans, who emulate the happiness of the gods, within the limits imposed by human nature. "Epicurus said that he was prepared to compete with Zeus in happiness, as long as he had a barley cake and some water."[4]

If, however, the gods are as independent as this conception indicates, then they will not observe the sacrifices we make to them, and Epicurus was indeed widely regarded as undermining the foundations of traditional religion. Furthermore, how can Epicurus explain the visions that we receive of the gods, if the gods don't deliberately send them to us? These visions, replies Epicurus, are material images travelling through the world, like everything else that we see or imagine, and are therefore something real; they travel through the world because of the general laws

4. Aelian, *Miscellaneous Histories*, 4.13 (text 159).

of atomic motion, not because god sends them. But then what sort of bodies must the gods have, if these images are always streaming off them, and yet they remain strong and invulnerable? Their bodies, replies Epicurus, are continually replenished by images streaming towards them; indeed the 'body' of a god may be nothing more than a focus to which the images travel, the images that later travel to us and make up our conception of its nature.[5]

If the gods do not exert themselves for our benefit, how is it that the world around us is suitable for our habitation? It happened by accident, said Epicurus, an answer that gave ancient critics ample opportunity for ridicule, and yet it makes him a thinker of a very modern sort, well ahead of his time. Epicurus believed that the universe is a material system governed by the laws of matter. The fundamental elements of matter are atoms,[6] which move, collide, and form larger structures according to physical laws. These larger structures can sometimes develop into yet larger structures by the addition of more matter, and sometimes whole worlds will develop. These worlds are extremely numerous and variable; some will be unstable, but others will be stable. The stable ones will persist and give the appearance of being designed to be stable, like our world, and living structures will sometimes develop out of the elements of these worlds. This theory is no longer as unbelievable as it was to the non-Epicurean scientists and philosophers of the ancient world, and its broad outlines may well be true.

We happen to have a great deal of evidence about the Epicurean philosophy of nature, which served as a philosophical foundation for the rest of the system. But many Epicureans would have had little interest in this subject, nor did they need to, if their curiosity or scepticism did not drive them to ask fundamental questions. What was most important in Epicurus' philosophy of nature was the overall conviction that our life on this earth comes with no strings attached; that there is no Maker whose puppets we are; that there is no script for us to follow and be constrained by; that it is up to us to discover the real constraints which our own nature imposes on us. When we do this, we find something very delightful: life is free, life is good, happiness is possible, and we can enjoy the bliss of the gods, rather than abasing ourselves to our misconceptions of them.

5. This is only a suggestion; it is not easy to understand the Epicurean conception of the nature of the gods, and readers should be aware that modern scholars do not agree about the correct interpretation of the evidence.

6. He borrowed this hypothesis from Democritus, an earlier atomist, and it was borrowed in turn from Epicurus by Pierre Gassendi, who introduced the atomic theory into modern science in the seventeenth century.

To say that life is free is not to say that we don't need to observe any moral constraints. It is a very bad plan to cheat on your friends or assault people in the street or do anything else that would cause you to worry about their reactions. Why is this a bad plan? Not because god has decreed that such things are 'immoral', but because it is stupid to do anything that would cause you to worry about anything. In the view of some moral philosophers (both ancient and modern) this view makes Epicureanism an immoral philosophy, because it denies that there is anything intrinsically wrong with immoral conduct. If we could be sure that nobody would find out, then we would have no reason to worry about the consequences, and therefore no reason not to be immoral. True, admits Epicurus, but we can never be sure that nobody will find out, and so the most tranquil course is to obey the rules of social morality quite strictly. These have been developed over the centuries for quite understandable reasons, mostly to give ourselves mutual protection against hostile animals and people. The legal and moral rules of society serve a good purpose, although it is not worthwhile to exert yourself to become prominent in public affairs and have the anxiety of public office. Much more satisfying and valuable is to develop individual relationships of mutual confidence, for a friend will come to your assistance when an ordinary member of the public will not. In fact, friends are our most important defence against insecurity and are our greatest sources of strength, after the truths of Epicurean philosophy itself.

Friends and philosophy are the two greatest resources available to help us live our lives in confidence and without anxiety. Perhaps the best thing of all would be to have friends who shared our Epicurean philosophy with us; many Epicureans lived in small Epicurean communities, as did the followers of Pythagoras in earlier times. These Epicurean communities were probably modelled on the community that Epicurus established on the outskirts of Athens, called "The Garden." We know very little about the organization of these communities, except that they did not require their members to give up their private property to the commune (unlike the Pythagoreans and some modern religious cults) and that they probably involved regular lessons or discussions of Epicurean philosophy. They also included household servants and women on equal terms with the men, which was completely out of line with the social norms of the time, but Epicurus believed that humble people and women could understand and benefit from his philosophy as well as educated men, another respect in which Epicurean philosophy was well ahead of its time.

The membership of women caused scandalous rumours, spread by hostile sources, that "The Garden" was a place for continuous orgies and parties, rumours apparently supported by Epicurus' thesis that bodily pleasure is the original and basic form of pleasure. But Epicurus believed in marriage and the family, for those who are ready for the responsibility, and he disapproved of sexual love, because it ensnares the lover in tangles of unnecessary needs and vulnerabilities. Here's the typical pattern: first lust, then infatuation, then consummation, then jealousy or boredom. There's only anxiety and distress in this endlessly repeated story, except for the sex itself, and Epicurus regarded sex as an unnecessary pleasure, which never did anybody any real good—count yourself lucky if it does you no harm![7] There is nothing intrinsically wrong with casual sex, but much more important than either love or sex is friendship, which "dances around the world, announcing to all of us that we must wake up to blessedness."[8]

One of the remarkable features of Epicurus' philosophy is that it can be understood at several levels of subtlety. You don't need to be a philosophical genius to grasp the main points, which is why Epicurus coined slogans and maxims for ordinary people to memorize, to help them relieve their anxiety whenever it might arise. There were signet rings and hand mirrors, for example, engraved with the words 'death is nothing', so the faithful could be reminded while going about their daily business. Suppose, though, that you're not convinced that 'death is nothing', for example, and you want proof before you organize your life around that idea. For people like you, Epicurus wrote letters outlining his basic arguments, which circulated freely among those interested in the topic. Suppose, again, that you already have a philosophical education, and you want to assess Epicurus' arguments against the competing arguments, from other philosophers, for example. For this purpose he wrote elaborately careful and thorough memoranda of his arguments; his main treatise on natural philosophy ran to a staggering thirty-seven volumes. This extremely long book was given an intermediate (but still quite detailed) summary by Epicurus, and there may have been other levels of length and subtlety. If on a certain topic all our evidence seems superficial, that is probably because the more extensive discussions of that topic have not survived.

* * * * *

7. Diogenes Laertius, *Lives and Sayings of Famous Philosophers* x.118 (text 8).
8. Epicurus, *Vatican Sayings* (text 6) #52; cf. *Principal Doctrines* (text 5) #27.

Modern students of Epicureanism should know the status of the available evidence. None of Epicurus' major works survives in its entirety, but of his many abbreviations and summaries, three survive because they are quoted in *Lives and Sayings of Famous Philosophers*, by Diogenes Laertius, an otherwise unknown third-century-A.D. compiler. The most important of these is the *Letter to Menoeceus* (text 4), which gives the basic outline of the Epicurean approach to personal happiness. The *Letter to Herodotus* (text 2) gives the basic outline of the Epicurean materialist philosophy of nature, and the *Letter to Pythocles* (text 3) concerns the natural phenomena of the sky (which many felt were the work of the gods). These letters can be trusted to reflect Epicurus' own views and way of arguing, as can the so-called "Principal Doctrines" (text 5), a group of forty short and pithy remarks, which were collected so that the basic principles of the Epicurean system could be easily memorized. A similar collection, the so-called "Vatican Sayings" (text 6), is a mixture of sayings from Epicurus and other Epicureans, and we print the sayings that seem likely to have come from Epicurus himself.

The picture that emerges from this evidence can be somewhat enlarged with fragments from Epicurus' works. In some cases, these are literally fragments, charred and brittle pieces of papyrus (the ancient equivalent of writing paper) excavated from a villa in Herculaneum which was engulfed by the eruption of Mt. Vesuvius in A.D. 79. Their damaged state explains the numerous gaps ('lacunae') in our text of part of Book 25 of Epicurus' *On Nature* (text 34). Other fragments are small portions of Epicurus' works quoted by other Epicurean writers, such as Philodemus of Gadara, whose charred books were also found in Herculaneum. Still other fragments are small portions of Epicurus' works quoted by other ancient authors whose works survived in the ordinary way, by being copied from handwritten book to handwritten book. Sometimes the source tells us which treatise or letter he is quoting from (texts 30 to 64). In other cases we cannot know what work the quotation comes from (texts 65 to 159).

Not all quotations can be taken to be accurate, word-for-word citations from Epicurus. We have indicated, by using quotation marks, where we thought the source was purporting to quote Epicurus, but ancient standards of accuracy were not as rigorous as modern ones, especially when ancient writers were attacking their intellectual enemies. Other sources don't even purport to quote Epicurus' exact words, and we need to be yet more careful with these reports, which are referred to as 'testimonia'. Readers should regard purported quotations as generally more reliable than testimonia, but should always prefer Epicurus' own texts to both these other kinds of evidence. Fortunately, most of the evidence coheres, and it is usually possible to reach a reasonable assessment of Epicurus' views, at least on the topics where evidence is available.

We also have long discussions of Epicureanism from the pen of the well-known philosopher Cicero, who discussed Epicureanism in several of his books (texts 15 to 26). Cicero was not himself an Epicurean, and he was content to rely on Epicurean handbooks of a period close to his time. Sometimes Cicero does not really understand what he is transmitting (though that doesn't stop him from arguing against it), and in these cases especially we can be confident that he is faithfully paraphrasing his Epicurean source. But what he transmits is only what he selects from his Epicurean source, and his source is not Epicurus himself but a later (more or less orthodox) follower. Plutarch, another well-known philosopher, was a more scholarly—and a more hostile—critic, who argued against the Epicurean philosophy with all the devices of argument (legitimate and illegitimate) at his command. There are more quotations from Epicurus in Plutarch than in Cicero, but the Epicurean way of thinking is more distorted, because Plutarch's purpose is to ridicule it, by belittling it element by element. The most useful evidence from Plutarch comes in his attack on the book written by Colotes, an early follower of Epicurus (text 29), but there is evidence also in his critique of the self-effacing Epicurean life-style, *Is 'Live inconspicuously' a wise precept?*, and in his polemical essay called *It is quite impossible to enjoy life on Epicurean principles*.

By far the most useful body of evidence that is *not* transmitted in our *Reader* is a poem by Lucretius, a Roman Epicurean of the first half of the first century B.C. This is a long didactic poem in six books, called *De Rerum Natura* (*On the Nature of Things*), which sets out in Latin verse the Epicurean philosophy of nature, drawing an occasional liberating and antisuperstitious lesson. It is a classic of world literature, which impresses as much by its rich poetic qualities as by the rigour of its thought. But it is not possible to know exactly how reliable it is as a source for the views of Epicurus, since the so-called *Major Summary* (a detailed summary of Epicurus' thirty-seven-volume *On Nature*), on which it seems to have been based, has entirely perished. We print two particularly important passages which do seem to have been drawn quite directly from Epicurus' own works (texts 27 and 28), but probably most of Lucretius' poem reflects Epicurus' views equally well. A good example is Book III, lines 830–1094, which offers the arguments for believing that 'death is nothing to us'; although we cannot be certain that Lucretius is not introducing new ideas, there is nothing here that is incompatible with Epicurus' known views. A comprehensive study of Epicureanism would include Lucretius among its main body of evidence, and we recommend that our readers read it in the bilingual Loeb Classical Library edition, with a translation by W.H.D. Rouse, revised by M. F. Smith (second edition, revised 1992).

* * * * *

Epicurus developed a system of philosophy and a way of living that deserve our respect and understanding, perhaps even our allegiance. This way of living claimed many thousands of committed followers, all over the ancient Mediterranean world, in cooperative communities that lasted for hundreds of years. But from the very beginning of his teaching mission, his message was opposed and distorted, first by academic philosophers and political authorities, and later by Christians. Epicureans apparently almost never switched their allegiance to other philosophical systems, whereas other schools regularly lost students to the Epicureans. Why? Perhaps because the Epicureans found that their system made excellent sense. But the explanation offered by Arcesilaus, Epicurus' rival, is typically dismissive: "You can turn a man into a eunuch, but you can't turn a eunuch into a man."[9] Even in modern times, the critics of Epicureanism continue to misrepresent it as a lazy-minded, shallow, pleasure-loving, immoral, or godless travesty of real philosophy. In our day the word 'epicureanism' has come to mean its opposite—a pretentious enthusiasm for rare and expensive food and drink. Please have the courage to ignore two thousand years of negative prejudice, and assess this philosophy on its own considerable merits. This book gives you the evidence you need.

D. S. Hutchinson
Trinity College
University of Toronto

9. Diogenes Laertius, *Lives and Sayings of Famous Philosophers* iv.43. Arcesilaus was the Head of the Platonic Academy in Epicurus' day.

Suggestions for further reading

E. Asmis *Epicurus' Scientific Method* Ithaca and London 1984.
D. Clay *Lucretius and Epicurus* Ithaca and London 1983.
W. Englert *Epicurus on the Swerve and Voluntary Action* Atlanta 1987.
H. Jones *The Epicurean Tradition* London 1989.
A. A. Long *Hellenistic Philosophy* ed. 2 London/Berkeley/Los Angeles 1986.
A. A. Long and D. N. Sedley *The Hellenistic Philosophers* Cambridge 1987.
P. Mitsis *Epicurus' Ethical Theory* Ithaca and London 1988.
J. M. Rist *Epicurus: An Introduction* Cambridge 1972.

Sources

H. Usener *Epicurea* Leipzig 1887.
G. Arrighetti *Epicuro: Opere* ed. 2 Turin 1973.
Lucretius *De Rerum Natura* tr. W.H.D. Rouse; rev. ed. M. F. Smith, Cambridge and London 1982.

Abbreviations

A:	G. Arrighetti, *Epicuro Opere*
CIAG:	*Commentaria in Aristotelem Graeca*
Dox. Gr.:	*Doxographi Graeci*, ed. H. Diels
M:	Sextus Empiricus, *Adversus Mathematicos*
PH:	Sextus Empiricus, *Outlines of Pyrrhonism*
Prep. Ev.:	Eusebius, *Preparatio Evangelica*
SVF:	*Stoicorum Veterum Fragmenta*, ed. H. von Arnim
U:	H. Usener, *Epicurea*
W-H:	C. Wachsmuth and O. Hense, edd., Stobaeus Anthology

The Epicurus Reader

The ancient biography of Epicurus

TEXT 1: *The Life of Epicurus:* Diogenes Laertius 10.1–16 (selections)

1. Epicurus, son of Neocles and Chairestrate, was an Athenian citizen of the deme Gargettus and of the clan Philaidae, according to Metrodorus in his *On Noble Birth.* It is said, especially by Heracleides in his summary of Sotion, that he was raised on Samos after the Athenians sent colonists there; that at eighteen years of age he went to Athens, when Xenocrates was in [charge of] the Academy and Aristotle was spending time in Chalcis; that he went to join his father in Colophon when Alexander of Macedon had died and Perdiccas expelled the Athenians [from Samos]; 2. that he spent some time there and gathered students around him, then returned to Athens again in the archonship of Anaxicrates [307–306 B.C.]; and that up to a certain time he philosophized in conjunction with the others, but later developed the system which bears his name and taught his own distinctive views.

He himself says that he began to practice philosophy when he was fourteen years old. Apollodorus the Epicurean says, in book one of his *Life of Epicurus,* that he turned to philosophy because he was contemptuous of the school-teachers for not being able to interpret for him the [lines about] chaos in Hesiod. Hermippus says that he had been a grammar teacher, but then came across Democritus' treatises and threw himself headlong into philosophy. . . . 9. . . . . There is abundant evidence of the fellow's unsurpassed kindness to all men: his country honoured him with bronze statues; his friends were so numerous that they could not be counted by entire cities; all his followers were transfixed by the siren-song of his teachings, except Metrodorus of Stratonicea, who went over to Carneades, overburdened perhaps by his unsurpassed acts of goodness; though nearly all the others have died out, his succession has always persisted, one student following another in a numberless sequence of leaders; 10. and [there is] his gratitude to his parents, kindness to his brothers, and gentleness to his servants, as is clear both from the provisions of his will and from the fact that they joined him in philosophizing, the most notable being the aforementioned Mus; in a word, he was a friend to all mankind. His piety to the gods and love for his country were too great for words. So gentlemanly was he that he did not even participate in political life. And despite the severely troubled times then afflicting Greece, he lived out his life there, travelling through Ionia two or three times to see friends. And friends came to him from all over, and lived with him in the Garden (as Apollodorus too says); and he bought it for eighty minas.

11. Diocles says in book three of his summary that they lived very simply and frugally. "At any rate," he says, "they were content with a half-pint serving of weak wine and generally their drink was water." And that Epicurus did not think it right to put one's possessions into a common fund, as did Pythagoras who said "friends' possessions are common"; for that sort of thing is a mark of mistrust; and if there is mistrust there is no friendship. In his letters he himself says that he is content with just water and simple bread. And he says, "Send me a little pot of cheese so that I can indulge in extravagance when I wish." This was the character of the man who taught that pleasure is the goal. . . .

12. . . . According to Diocles he was most impressed by Anaxagoras among earlier philosophers, although he opposed him on some points, and by Archelaus, Socrates' teacher. He used to train his followers, [Diocles] says, even to memorize his treatises.

13. Apollodorus in his *Chronology* says that he studied under Nausiphanes and Praxiphanes. He himself denies it, and says in the letter to Eurylochus that he is self-taught. He denies that there ever was a philosopher named Leucippus, and so does Hermarchus; some, including Apollodorus the Epicurean, say that Leucippus was Democritus' teacher. Demetrius of Magnesia says that he studied under Xenocrates too. . . .

14. . . . Ariston says in his life of Epicurus that he copied the *Canon* straight out of the *Tripod* of Nausiphanes, under whom he also says he studied, in addition to Pamphilus the Platonist in Samos. And that he began to philosophize at the age of twelve and founded his school at the age of 32.

He was born, according to Apollodorus in his *Chronology*, in the third year of the 109th Olympiad, in the archonship of Sosigenes [341 B.C.] on the seventh day of the month of Gamelion, seven years after Plato's death. **15.** When he was 32 he first founded a school in Mytilene and Lampsacus [and stayed] for five years. Then he moved to Athens and died there in the second year of the 127th Olympiad in the archonship of Pytharatus [271–270 B.C.], at the age of 72. Hermarchus, son of Agemortus, of Mytilene, took over the school.

He died of kidney stones, as Hermarchus too says in his letters, after an illness of fourteen days. At that point, as Hermippus also says, he got into a bronze bathtub filled with warm water, asked for unmixed wine, and tossed it back. **16.** He then bade his friends to remember his teachings and died thus.

The extant letters

The following three letters are preserved because Diogenes Laertius included them in his biography. They are the most important surviving evidence for the philosophy of Epicurus. The *Letter to Herodotus* (text 2) is a summary of physical doctrine; the *Letter to Menoeceus* (text 4) is an even briefer summary of ethics; the authenticity of the summary of meteorology in text 3 (*Letter to Pythocles*) has been questioned, but we regard it as genuine.

TEXT 2: *Letter to Herodotus:* Diogenes Laertius 10.34–83

34. Epicurus to Herodotus, greetings:
35. For the sake of those, Herodotus, who are unable to work out with precision each and every detail of what we have written on nature and who lack the ability to work through the longer books I have composed, I have myself prepared an adequate summary of the entire system, to facilitate the firm memorization of the most general doctrines, in order that at each and every opportunity they may be able to help themselves in the most important issues, to the degree that they retain their grasp on the study of nature. Even those well advanced in the examination of the universe must recall the outline of the entire system; and this outline is structured according to basic principles. For we frequently need the overall application [of the intellect], but not so often the detailed application.
36. We must, then, approach those [general points] continually, and get into our memory an amount [of doctrine] sufficient to permit the most vital application [of the intellect] to the facts; moreover, complete precision on detailed points will be discovered if the general outlines are comprehensively grasped and remembered. For even the fully expert [student of physics] gets as the most vital benefit of complete precision the ability to make nimble use of his applications, and ‹this would happen if every point› were united in [a set of] simple principles and maxims. For it is not possible to know the concentrated result of our continuous overview of the universe unless one can have in oneself a comprehensive grasp by means of brief maxims of all that might also be worked out in detail with precision.

37. Since this kind of method is useful to *all* those who are concerned with the study of nature, I recommend constant activity in the study of nature; and with this sort of activity more than any other I bring calm to my life. That is why I have composed for you this type of summary statement of the basic principles of the entire set of doctrines.

First, Herodotus, we need to have grasped what is denoted by our words, [1] so that by referring to what they denote we can make decisions about the objects of opinion, investigation, or puzzlement and [2] so that all of these things will not remain undecided, [as they would] if we tried to give an infinitely long demonstration, and [3] so that our words will not be empty. 38. For it is necessary that we look to the primary conception corresponding to each word and that it stand in no need of demonstration, if, that is, we are going to have something to which we can refer the object of search or puzzlement and opinion. Again, it is also necessary to observe all things in accordance with one's sense-perceptions, i.e., simply according to the present applications, whether of the intellect or of any other of the criteria, and similarly [to observe everything] in accordance with our actual feelings, so that we can have some sign by which we may make inferences both about what awaits confirmation and about the non-evident.

After distinguishing these points we must next arrive at a general view about the things which are non-evident. The first point is that nothing comes into being from what is not; for [in that case] everything would be coming into being from everything, with no need of seeds. 39. And if that which disappears were destroyed into what is not, all things would have been destroyed, since that into which they were dissolved does not exist. Further, the totality [of things] has always been just like it is now and always will be. For there is nothing for it to change into. For there exists nothing in addition to the totality, which could enter into it and produce the change.

Moreover,[1] the totality is [made up of] ‹bodies and void›; for in all cases sense-perception itself testifies that bodies exist, and it is by sense-perception that we must infer by reasoning what is non-evident, as I already said. 40. And if there did not exist that which we call void and space and intangible nature, bodies would not have any place to be in or move through, as they obviously do move. Beyond these two things [viz. bodies and void] nothing can be conceived, either by a comprehensive grasp or analogously to things so grasped, [at least not if we mean]

---

1. A scholiast in antiquity added: "He makes this point in the *Major Summary* at the beginning and in book one of the *On Nature.*"

grasped as complete natures rather than as what are termed properties or accidents of these [two] things.

Further, among[2] bodies, some are compounds, and some are those things from which compounds have been made. **41.** And these are atomic and unchangeable, if indeed they are not all going to be destroyed into not being but will remain firmly during the dissolutions of compounds, being full by nature and not being subject to dissolution in any way or fashion. Consequently the principles of bodies must be atomic natures.

Moreover, the totality is unlimited. For what is limited has an extreme; but an extreme is seen in contrast to something else, so that since it has no extreme it has no limit. But since it has no limit it would be unlimited and not limited.

Further, the totality is unlimited in respect of the number of bodies and the magnitude of the void. **42.** For if the void were unlimited and bodies limited, bodies would not come to a standstill anywhere but would move in scattered fashion throughout the unlimited void, since they would lack anything to support them or check them by collision. But if the void were limited, the unlimited bodies would not have a place to be in.

In addition, the bodies which are atomic and full, from which compounds both come to be and into which they are dissolved, are ungraspable when it comes to the differences among their shapes. For it is not possible that so many differences [in things] should come to be from the same shapes having been comprehensively grasped. And for each type of shape there is, quite simply, an unlimited number of similar [atoms], but with respect to the differences they are not quite simply unlimited but only ungraspable.

43.[3] And the atoms move continuously[4] for all time, some recoiling far apart from one another [upon collision], and others, by contrast, maintaining a [constant] vibration when they are locked into a compound or enclosed by the surrounding [atoms of a compound]. **44.** This is the re-

---

2. The scholiast adds: "This is also in book one of the *On Nature* and in books fourteen and fifteen, as well as in the *Major Summary*."

3. Scholiast: "A bit later he also says that division does not go on indefinitely; and he says since the qualities change, unless one intends simply to extend them indefinitely with respect to their magnitudes too." This scholion is probably corrupt, and the sense is unclear.

4. Scholiast: "and he says a bit later that they also move with equal speed since the void gives an equal yielding [i.e., lack of resistance] to the lightest and to the heaviest."

sult of the nature of the void which separates each of them and is not able to provide any resistance; and their actual solidity causes their rebound vibration to extend, during the collision, as far as the distance which the entanglement [of the compound] permits after the collision.

There is no principle for these [entities], since the atoms and the void are eternal.[5] **45.** If all these points are remembered, a maxim as brief as this will provide an adequate outline for [developing] our conceptions about the nature of what exists.

Moreover, there is an unlimited number of cosmoi, and some are similar to this one and some are dissimilar. For the atoms, which are unlimited (as was shown just now), are also carried away to very remote distances. For atoms of the sort from which a world might come to be or by which it might be made are not exhausted [in the production] of one world or any finite number of them, neither worlds like this one nor worlds unlike them. Consequently, there is no obstacle to the unlimitedness of worlds.

46. Further, there exist outlines [i.e., images, *eidola*] which are similar in shape to solids, only much finer than observed objects. For it is not impossible for such compounds to come into being in the surrounding environment, nor that there should be favourable opportunities for the production of hollow and thin [films], nor that effluences should retain the relative position and standing [i.e., order] that they had in the solid objects. These outlines we call 'images'. Further, since their movement through the void occurs with no conflict from [atoms which] could resist them, it can cover any comprehensively graspable distance in an inconceivably [short] time. For the presence and absence of resistance takes on a similarity to slowness and speed.

47. The moving body itself, however, cannot reach several places at the same time, speaking in terms of time contemplated by reason; for that is unthinkable. Yet when considered as arriving in perceptible time from any point at all in the unlimited, it will not be departing from the place from which we comprehensively grasp its motion as having come from. For it will be like resistance even if to this point we leave the speed of the movement free from resistance. The retention of this basic principle too is useful.

5. Scholiast: "He says a bit later that there are not even any qualities in atoms, except shape and size and weight; in the *Twelve Basic Principles* he says that their colour changes according to the arrangement of the atoms; and that they cannot have every magnitude—at any rate an atom has never been seen with sense-perception."

Next, none of the appearances testifies against [the theory] that the images have an unsurpassed fineness; and that is why they have unsurpassed speed too, since they find every passage suitably sized for there being no or few [bodies] to resist their flow, whereas there is some [body] to resist a large or infinite number of atoms.

48. In addition, [none of the facts testifies against the claim] that the production of images occurs as fast as thought. For there is a continuous flow from the surface of bodies, though it is not obvious from any reduction in bulk because the [objects are] refilled [by other atoms]; [and this flow] preserves for quite some time the position and order of the atoms which it had in the solid, even if it is sometimes disrupted; and [two-dimensional] compounds are quickly produced in the surrounding environment, since they do not need to be filled out with depth—and there are certain other ways in which such natures [i.e., compound images] can be produced. None of these [claims] is testified against by the senses, providing one considers the clear facts in a certain way; one will also refer to [the senses] the [fact that] harmonious sets [of qualities] come to us from external objects.

49. One must also believe that it is when something from the external objects enters into us that we see and think about their shapes. For external objects would not stamp into us the nature of their own colour and shape via the air which is between us and them, nor via the rays or any kind of flows which move from us to them, as well as [they would] by means of certain outlines which share the colour and shape of the objects and enter into us from them, entering the vision or the intellect according to the size and fit [of the effluences] and moving very quickly; **50.** then, for this reason, they give the presentation of a single, continuous thing, and preserve the harmonious set [of qualities] generated by the external object, as a result of the coordinate impact from that object [on us], which [in turn] originates in the vibration of the atoms deep inside the solid object. And whatever presentation we receive by a form of application, whether by the intellect or by the sense organs, and whether of a shape or of accidents, this *is* the shape of the solid object, produced by the continuous compacting or residue of the image. Falsehood or error *always* resides in the added opinion ⟨in the case of something which awaits⟩ testimony for or against it but in the event receives neither supporting testimony ⟨nor opposing testimony⟩.[6]

51. For the similarity of appearances (which are like what are grasped in a representational picture and occur either in dreams or in some other

6. Scholiast: "According to a certain motion in ourselves which is linked to the application to presentations but is distinct, according to which falsehood occurs."

applications of the intellect or the other criteria) to what are called real and true things would never occur if some such thing were not added [to the basic experience]. And error would not occur if we did not have some other motion too in ourselves which is linked ‹to the application to presentations› but is distinct; falsehood occurs because of this, if it is not testified for or is testified against; but if it is testified for or is not testified against, truth occurs.

52. One must, then, keep this doctrine too quite firmly in mind, in order to avoid destroying the criteria of clear facts and to avoid having error placed on an equal basis with that which has been established, which would confound everything.

Moreover, hearing too occurs when a flow moves from that object which makes an utterance or produces a sound or makes a noise or in any other way causes the auditory experience. This flow is broken into small masses which are homogeneous with the whole which at the same time preserve an harmonious set [of qualities] relative to each other and also a unique kind of unity which extends back to the originating source and, usually, produces the perceptual experience occasioned by the flow; and if not, it only makes the external object apparent. 53. For without some harmonious set [of qualities] coming from there, this sort of perceptual experience could not occur. So one must not think that the air itself is shaped by the emitted voice or even by things of like character— for it is far from being the case that it [i.e., air] is affected in this way by that [i.e., voice]—but rather when we emit voice the blow which occurs inside us precipitates the expulsion of certain masses which produce a flow similar to breath, and which causes in us the auditory experience.

Further, one must also believe that the [sense of] smell, like hearing too, would never have produced any experience if there were not certain masses moving from the object and being commensurate for the stimulation of this sense organ, some of them of one sort, i.e., disturbing and uncongenial, and some of another, i.e., non-disturbing and congenial [to the organ of smell].

54. Further, one must believe that the atoms bring with them none of the qualities of things which appear except shape, weight, and size and the [properties] which necessarily accompany shape. For every quality changes, while the atoms do not change in any respect; for it is necessary that during the dissolution of compounds something should remain solid and undissolved, which will guarantee that the changes are not into what is not nor from what is not, but come about by rearrangements in many cases, and in some cases too by additions and subtractions [of atoms from the compound]. That is why it is necessary that the things which are rearranged should be indestructible and not have the nature of what

changes, but rather their own masses and configurations. For it is also necessary that these things should remain [unchanged].

55. For even with things in our experience which change their shapes by the removal [of matter], the shape is grasped as inhering in the object which changes, while its qualities do not so inhere. The shape remains, but the qualities are eliminated from the entire body. So these features which are left behind [after a change] are sufficient to produce the differences in compounds, since it *is* necessary that some things be left behind and that there not be a destruction into what is not.

Moreover, one should not believe that atoms have every [possible] magnitude, so that one may avoid being testified against by the appearances. But one should believe that there are some differences in magnitude. For if this [doctrine] is added, then it will be easier to account for what, according to our feelings and sense-perceptions, actually happens. 56. But [to suppose] that *every* magnitude exists is not useful for [accounting for] the differences of qualities, and at the same time it would be necessary that some atoms reach the point of being visible to us—which is not seen to occur nor can one conceive how an atom could become visible.

In addition to these points, one must not believe that there can be an unlimited number of masses—no matter how small—in any finite body. Consequently, not only must one eliminate unlimited division into smaller pieces (to avoid making everything weak and being forced in our comprehensive grasps of compound things to exhaust the things which exist by reducing them to non-existence), but one must also not believe that within finite bodies there is an unlimited movement, not even by smaller and smaller stages.

57. For as soon as one says that there is in some thing an unlimited number of masses, no matter how small, then one cannot think how this magnitude could any longer be limited. For obviously these unlimited masses must be of some size or other; and no matter how small they might be, the magnitude [of the whole object] would for all that be unlimited. And since the limited has an extreme which can be distinguished even if it cannot be observed on its own, it is impossible not to conceive that the thing next to it is of the same character and that by moving forward from one point to the next in this fashion it turns out that one will in this fashion reach the unlimited conceptually.

58. And we must conceive that the minimal perceptible [part] is neither such as to be traversible nor is it totally and altogether unlike this. It has something in common with things which permit of being traversed, but [unlike them] it does not permit the distinguishing of parts [within it]; but whenever, because of the resemblance created by what they have in

common, we think that we are going to distinguish some [part] of it—one part here, another over there—it must be that we encounter something of equal size. We observe these one after another, starting from the first, and not [as being] in the same place nor as touching each other's parts with their own, but rather we [see] them measuring out magnitudes in their own unique way, more of them measuring out a larger magnitude and fewer of them a smaller.

One must believe that the minimal part in the atom also stands in this relation. 59. It is obvious that it is only in its smallness that it differs from what is observed in the case of perception, but it does stand in the same relation. For indeed it is because of this relation that we have already asserted that the atom has magnitude, and have merely extended it far beyond [perceptible things] in smallness. And again we must believe that the minimal and indivisible parts are limits which provide from themselves as primary [units] a standard of measurement for the lengths of larger and smaller [atoms], when we contemplate invisible things with reason. For what they have in common with things which do not permit of movement [across themselves] is enough to get us this far; but it is not possible for these [minimal parts] to possess motion and so move together [into compounds].

60. Further, one must not assert that the unlimited has an up and a down in the sense of an [absolutely] highest and lowest point. We know, however, that what is over our heads from wherever we stand, or what is below any point which we think of—it being possible to project both indefinitely—will never appear to us as being at the same time and in the same respect both up and down. For it is impossible to conceive of this. Consequently, it is possible to grasp as one motion the one conceived of as indefinitely [extended] upwards and the one conceived of as indefinitely [extended] downwards, even if a thousand times over a thing moving from us towards the places over our heads should arrive at the feet of those above us or a thing moving from us downwards should arrive at the head of those below us.

61. Furthermore, it is necessary that the atoms move at equal speed, when they move through the void and nothing resists them. For heavy things will not move faster than small and light ones, *when*, that is, nothing stands in their way; nor do small things move faster than large ones, since they all have a passage commensurate to them, when, that is, nothing resists these atoms either; nor is upward [movement] faster; neither is the sideways [movement] produced by collisions faster; nor is the downward [movement] caused by their own weight faster either. For as long as either ‹of them› prevails, the motion will continue as fast as thought,

until it meets with resistance, either from an external source or from its own weight counteracting the force of a colliding body.

62. Moreover, with respect to compounds, some will move faster than others, though the atoms [by themselves] move at equal speed, because the atoms in aggregates are moving towards one place [i.e., in the same direction] in the shortest continuous time, even if they do not do so in the [units of] time which reason can contemplate; but they frequently collide, until the continuity of the motion becomes perceptible. For the added opinion concerning the invisible—i.e., that the [units of] time which reason can contemplate will allow for continuous motion—is not true in such cases. For everything that is observed or grasped by the intellect in an [act of] application is true.

63. Next, one must see, by making reference to our sense-perceptions and feelings (for these will provide the most secure conviction), that the soul is a body [made up of] fine parts distributed throughout the entire aggregate, and most closely resembling breath with a certain admixture of heat, in one way resembling breath and in another resembling heat. There is also the ‹third› part which is much finer than even these [components] and because of this is more closely in harmony with the rest of the aggregate too. All of this is revealed by the abilities of the soul, its feelings, its ease of motion, its thought processes, and the things whose removal leads to our death.

Further, one must hold firmly that the soul is most responsible for sense-perception. 64. But [the soul] would not have acquired this [power] if it were not somehow enclosed by the rest of the aggregate. But the rest of the aggregate, though it provides for the soul this cause [of sense-perception], itself has a share in this property because of the soul; still it does not share in all the features [of sense-perception] which the soul has. That is why, when the soul has departed, it does not have sense-perception. For it could not have acquired this power all by itself, but something else which came into being with it provided body [with this power]; and this other thing, through the power actualized in itself by its motion, immediately produced for itself a property of sense-perception and then gave it (because of their close proximity and harmonious relationship) to the body too, as I said.

65. That is why the soul, as long as it is in [the body], will never lack sense-perception even if some other part has departed; but no matter what [parts] of it are destroyed along with the container's dissolution (whether entire or partial), if the soul survives it will be able to perceive. But the rest of the aggregate—whole or part—is not able to perceive even if it survives, when the number of atoms, however small it be, which makes up the nature of the soul, has departed.

Furthermore, when the entire aggregate is destroyed, the soul is scattered and no longer has the same powers, nor can it move; consequently, it does not then [in fact] have [the power of] sense-perception. **66.** For it is not possible to conceive of it as perceiving if it is not in this complex and not executing these movements, [i.e.,] when the containing and surrounding [parts] are not such as now contain it and make possible these motions.[7]

67. Moreover, one must also think of this, that we apply the term 'incorporeal', in the most common meaning of the term, to what could be conceived of as independently existing. But the incorporeal cannot be thought of as independently existing, except for the void. And the void can neither act nor be acted upon but merely provides [the possibility of] motion through itself for bodies. Consequently, those who say that the soul is incorporeal are speaking to no point. For if it were of that character, it could neither act nor be acted upon at all. But in fact both of these properties are clearly distinguished as belonging to the soul.

68. So, if one refers all of these calculations concerning the soul to the feelings and sense-perceptions, and remembers what was said at the outset, one will see the points comprehended in the outline with sufficient clarity to be able to work out the details from this basis with precision and certainty.

Further, the shapes and colours and sizes and weights and all the other things which are predicated of body as accidents, either of all [bodies] or of visible ones, and are known by sense-perception itself, these things must not be thought of as independent natures (for that is inconceivable). **69.** Nor [must it be thought] that they are altogether non-existent, nor that they are distinct incorporeal entities inhering in [the body], nor that they are parts of it. But [one should think] that the whole body throughout derives its own permanent nature from all of these [properties]—though not in such a way as to be a compound [of them], just as when a larger aggregate is produced from the masses themselves, whether the primary ones or magnitudes smaller than the whole object in question—but only, as I say, deriving its own permanent nature from all of these. But all of these [are known by] their own peculiar forms of application and comprehension, always in close accompaniment with the

---

7. Scholion: "Elsewhere he says that it is also composed of very smooth and very round atoms, differing quite a bit from those of fire. And that part of it is irrational, and is distributed throughout the rest of the body, while the rational part is in the chest, as is evident from [feelings of] fear and joy. And that sleep occurs when the parts of the soul which are distributed through the whole compound are fixed in place or spread apart and then collide because of the impacts. And semen comes from the entire body."

aggregate and in no way separated from it, which is given the predicate 'body' by reference to the aggregate conception.

70. Further, it often happens that some impermanent properties, which are neither invisible nor incorporeal, accompany bodies. Consequently, using this term in the commonest sense, we make it clear that the[se] properties neither have the nature of an entire thing, which we call a body when we grasp it in aggregate, nor the nature of the permanent accompaniments without which it is not possible to conceive of a body. They would all be referred to according to certain applications of the aggregate which accompanies [them]—71. but [only] when they are observed to inhere [in bodies], since the properties are not *permanent* accompaniments [of those bodies]. And we should not eliminate this clear evidence from what exists just because [the properties] do not have the nature of an entire thing which happens to be what we also call a body, nor the nature of the permanent accompaniments; but neither are they to be regarded as independent entities, since this is not conceivable either in their case or in the case of permanent accidents; but one must think that they are all, just as they appear [to be], properties somehow ⟨related to⟩ the bodies and not permanent accompaniments nor things which have the status of an independent nature. But they are observed just as sense-perception itself presents their peculiar traits.

72. Moreover, one must also think of this very carefully: one should not investigate time as we do the other things which we investigate in an object, [i.e.,] by referring to the basic grasps which are observed within ourselves, but we must reason [on the basis of] the clear experience according to which we utter [the phrases] "for a long time" or "for a short time" interpreting it in a manner closely connected [to our experience]. Nor must we alter the terms we use in order to 'improve' them, but we must apply the current terms to [time]; nor must one predicate anything else of it, as though it had the same substance as this peculiar thing—for there are people who do this. But the best policy is to reason solely by means of that which we associate with this peculiar thing and by which we measure it. 73. For this needs no demonstration, but [only] reasoning, because we associate it with days and nights and their parts, and similarly with the feelings too and with the absence of them, and with motions and states of rest, again, having in mind in connection with them precisely and only this peculiar property according to which we apply the term "time."[8]

On top of what has been said, one must believe that the cosmoi, and every finite compound which is similar in form to those which are fre-

8. Scholiast: "He also says this in book two of the *On Nature* and in the *Major Summary*."

quently seen, have come into being from the unlimited, all these things having been separated off from particular conglomerations [of matter], both larger and smaller; and that they are all dissolved again, some more quickly and some more slowly, and some undergoing this because of one kind of cause, some because of others.[9]

74. Again, one must not believe that the cosmoi necessarily have one kind of shape. . . . [10] For no one could demonstrate that a cosmos of one sort would not have included the sort of seeds from which animals, plants, and the rest of the observable things are formed as compounds, or that a [cosmos of a] different sort *could* not have [included the same things].[11]

75. Further, one must suppose that [human] nature was taught a large number of different lessons just by the facts themselves, and compelled [by them]; and that reasoning later made more precise what was handed over to it [by nature] and made additional discoveries—more quickly among some peoples, and more slowly among others and in some periods of time ‹making greater advances› and in others smaller ones.

Hence, names too did not originally come into being by convention, but the very natures of men, which undergo particular feelings and receive particular presentations according to the tribes they live in, expelled air in particular ways as determined by each of their feelings and presentations, in accordance too with the various local differences among their tribes. 76. And later [the names] were established by a general convention in each tribe, in order that their meanings might be less ambiguous for each other and might be expressed more succinctly. And those who were aware of certain previously unobserved things introduced them [to their tribes] and with them handed over certain words [for the things], some being forced to utter them, others choosing them by reasoning, following the commonest [mode of causation],[12] and communicated [their meaning] in this fashion.

---

9. Scholiast: "It is clear, then, that he says that the cosmoi are destructible, [this happening] when the parts undergo change. And elsewhere he says that the earth is supported by the air."

10. There is a lacuna at this point in the text. A scholiast adds: "But he himself says in book 12 of the *On Nature* that they are different: some are spherical, some egg-shaped, and others have different sorts of shapes; but they do not have every [possible] shape. Nor are they animals separated off from the unlimited."

11. Scholiast: "Similarly they are nourished in it. One must believe that it happens in the same way on earth too."

12. The text may be corrupt here; the sense should be that the inventors or discoverers followed an analogy with words already used in their own societies when deliberately coining new terms.

Moreover, when it comes to meteorological phenomena, one must believe that movements, turnings, eclipses, risings, settings, and related phenomena occur without any [god] helping out and ordaining or being about to ordain [things] and at the same time having complete blessedness and indestructibility; 77. for troubles and concerns and anger and gratitude are not consistent with blessedness, but these things involve weakness and fear and dependence on one's neighbours. Nor again can they be in possession of blessedness if they [the heavenly bodies] are at the same time balls of fire and adopt these movements by deliberate choice; rather, we must preserve the complete solemnity implied in all the terms applied to such conceptions, so that we do not generate from these terms opinions inconsistent with their solemnity; otherwise, the inconsistency itself will produce the greatest disturbance in our souls. Hence, one must hold the opinion that it is owing to the original inclusion of these compounds in the generation of the cosmos that this regularly recurring cycle too is produced.

78. Moreover, one must believe that it is the job of physics to work out precisely the cause of the most important things, and that blessedness lies in this part of meteorological knowledge and in knowing what the natures are which are observed in these meteorological phenomena, and all matters related to precision on this topic.

And again, [one must accept] that in such matters there is no room for things occurring in several ways and things which might occur otherwise, but that anything which suggests conflict or disturbance simply cannot occur in the indestructible and divine nature. And it is possible to grasp with the intellect that this is unqualifiedly so.

79. And what falls within the ambit of investigation into settings and risings and turnings, and eclipses and matters related to these, makes no further contribution to the blessedness which comes from knowledge; but people who know about these things, if they are ignorant of what the natures [in question] are and what the most important causes are, have fears just the same as if they did not have this special knowledge—and perhaps even more fears, since the wonderment which comes from the prior consideration of these phenomena cannot discover a resolution or the orderly management of the most important factors.

That is why even if we discover several causes for turnings and settings and risings and eclipses and things of this sort (as was also the case in [the investigation] of detailed occurrences) 80. we must not believe that our study of these matters has failed to achieve a degree of accuracy which contributes to our undisturbed and blessed state. Consequently, we should account for the causes of meteorological phenomena and everything which is non-evident, observing in how many different ways similar phenomena occur in our experience; and [we should] disdain those who fail to recognize what exists or comes to be in a single manner and what occurs in many different ways, because they overlook the [fact that the] presentation [comes] from great distances and are, moreover, ignorant of the circumstances in which one cannot achieve freedom from disturbance and those, similarly, in which one can achieve freedom from disturbance. So if we think that [a phenomenon] might also occur in some particular way and recognize the very fact that it [might] happen in many different ways, we shall be as free from disturbance as if we *knew* that it occurred in some particular way.

81. In addition to all these points in general, one must also conceive that the worst disturbance occurs in human souls [1] because of the opinion that these things [the heavenly phenomena] are blessed and indestructible and that they have wishes and undertake actions and exert causality in a manner inconsistent with those attributes, and [2] because of the eternal expectation and suspicion that something dreadful [might happen] such as the myths tell about, or [3] even because they fear that very lack of sense-perception which occurs in death, as though it were relevant to them, and [4] because they are not in this state as a result of their opinions but because of some irrational condition; hence, not setting a limit on their dread, they suffer a disturbance equal to or even greater than what they would suffer if they actually held these opinions. **82.** And freedom from disturbance is a release from all of this and involves a continuous recollection of the general and most important points [of the system].

Hence, one must attend to one's present feelings and sense-perceptions, to the common sense-perceptions for common properties and to the individual sense-perceptions for individual properties, and to every immediately clear fact as revealed by each of the criteria. For, if we attend to these things, we will give a correct and complete causal account of the source of our disturbance and fear, and [so] dissolve them, by accounting for the causes of meteorological and other phenomena which we are constantly exposed to and which terrify other men most severely.

Here, Herodotus, in summary form are the most important points about the nature of the universe; **83.** consequently, I think that this account, if mastered with precision, would be able to make a man incomparably stronger than other men, even if he does not go on to all of the precise details of individual doctrines. For he will also be able to clarify, by his own efforts, many of the precise details of individual doctrines in our entire system, and these points themselves, when lodged in memory, will be a constant aid.

For [these doctrines] are such that even those who have already worked out the details of individual doctrines sufficiently well or even completely, can, by analysing them into [intellectual] applications of this sort, acquire most of the [elements of the] survey of nature as a whole. But those who are not among the completely accomplished [students of nature] can, on the basis of these points and following the method which does not involve verbal expression, with the speed of thought achieve an overview of the doctrines most important for [achieving] tranquillity.

TEXT 3: *Letter to Pythocles:* Diogenes Laertius 10.83–116

83. Epicurus to Pythocles, greetings:

84. Cleon delivered to me your letter, in which you continued to display a good will to us worthy of our concern for you and tried, not unconvincingly, to recall the lines of reasoning which contribute to a blessed life; and you requested that I send you a brief and concise [statement of our] reasoning concerning meteorological phenomena in order to facilitate your recollections. For our other writings on the topic are hard to recall, even though, as you said, you have them constantly in hand. We were pleased to receive this request from you and were seized by pleasant expectations. 85. Therefore, having written all the rest, we shall produce what you requested, since these lines of reasoning will be useful to many others too, and especially to those who have just begun to sample true physics and those who are entangled in preoccupations more profound than some of the general studies. So grasp them well and, holding them keenly in your memory, survey them in conjunction with the rest [of my summary of physics], which I sent to Herodotus as the Smaller Summary.

First of all, do not believe that there is any other goal to be achieved by the knowledge of meteorological phenomena, whether they are discussed in conjunction with [physics in general] or on their own, than freedom from disturbance and a secure conviction, just as with the rest [of physics]. 86. [Our aim is] neither to achieve the impossible, even by force, nor to maintain a theory which is in all respects similar either to our discussions on the ways of life or to our clarifications of other questions in physics, such as the thesis that the totality [of things] consists of bodies and intangible nature, and that the elements are atomic, and all such things as are consistent with the phenomena in only one way. This is not the case with meteorological phenomena, but rather these phenomena admit of several different explanations for their coming to be and several different accounts of their existence which are consistent with our sense-perceptions.

For we should not do physics by following groundless postulates and stipulations, but in the manner called for by the phenomena; 87. for our life does not now need irrationality and groundless opinion, but rather for us to live without tumult. And everything happens smoothly and (providing everything is clarified by the method of several different explanations) consistently with the phenomena, when one accepts appropriately what is plausibly said about them. But when one accepts one theory and rejects another which is equally consistent with the phenomenon in question, it is clear that one has thereby blundered out of any sort of proper physics and fallen into mythology. Some of the phenomena which are within our [experience] and are observed just as they really are do provide signs applicable to what comes to pass in meteorology, but we cannot observe meteorological phenomena; for they can occur in several different ways. **88.** We must, however, observe the appearance of each thing and, with regard to the things connected with it, we must distinguish those whose coming to pass in several different ways is not testified against by what happens within our experience.

A cosmos is a circumscribed portion of the heavens which contains stars and an earth and all the phenomena, whose dissolution will involve the destruction of everything within it; it is separated off from the unlimited and terminates at a boundary which is either rare or dense; it is either revolving or stationary; it has an outline which is either round or triangular, or some shape or other. For all of these are possibilities. For none of the phenomena in this cosmos testifies against [these possibilities], since here it is not possible to grasp a limit [of our cosmos].

89. It is possible to grasp that there is an unlimited number of such cosmoi; and that such a cosmos can come into existence both within a[nother] cosmos and in an intercosmos, which is what we call the interval between cosmoi, in a place containing much void and not in an extensive area which is completely void, as some people say; [this happens] when certain seeds of the right sort rush in from one cosmos or intercosmos—or even from several—[thereby] gradually causing conjunctions and articulations and movements to another place (if it so happen) and influxes from [atoms] which are in the right condition, until [the cosmos] is completed and achieves stability, [i.e.,] for as long as the foundations laid can accept additional material. **90.** For one does not need just to have an aggregate come into being, or a rotation in the void in which a cosmos comes to be by necessity, as opinion holds, and [then] grows until it collides with another [cosmos], as one of the so-called physicists says. For this is in conflict with the phenomena.

The sun and the moon and the other heavenly bodies did not come into being on their own and then get included by the cosmos, but they immediately began to take shape and grow (and similarly for the earth and sea) by means of infusions and rotations of certain natures with fine parts, either breath-like or fiery or both. For sense-perception suggests that they [come into being] thus.

91. The size of the sun and the other heavenly bodies relative to us is just as big as it appears.[13] But relative to itself it is either bigger or a bit smaller than it is seen as being, or just the same size.[14] For in our experience too fire-signals, when seen from a distance, are observed in this way by our sense-perception. And every objection directed at this portion [of our theory] will be easily dissolved if only one pays attention to the clear facts, which we set out in our book *On Nature*. 92. The risings and settings of the sun and the moon and the other heavenly bodies could occur by kindling and extinguishing, as long as the circumstances in both locales [i.e., east and west] are such as to produce the aforementioned events; for none of the appearances testifies against this. ⟨And⟩ they could also be produced by the appearance [of these bodies] above the earth and a subsequent blocking [by it]; for none of the appearances testifies against this either. And it is not impossible that their motions come to pass because of the rotation of the entire cosmos, or by its rest and their rotation, produced by the necessity generated when they [first] rose, at the beginning when the cosmos was [first] coming into being. [There is probably a lacuna in the text here.] 93. . . . by extreme heat produced by a certain kind of distribution of the fire which constantly impinges on the adjoining places.

The turnings of the sun and moon could come to pass because of the obliquity of the heaven, which is compelled in this way at [certain] times; similarly, it could also be because of the resistance in the air, or because the fuel which regularly fits their requirements is burned up or is insufficient in quantity; or even because these heavenly bodies had forced on them from the very beginning the sort of rotation which causes them to have a kind of spiral motion. For all such possibilities and those like them are in no way inconsistent with any of the clear facts, providing one always in such detailed enquiries keeps a firm hold on what is possible and can refer each of them to what is consistent with the phenomena, not fearing the slavish technicalities of the astronomers.

94. The waning of the moon and its subsequent waxing could come to pass by means of the turning of this body and just as well by means of the changing shapes of the air, and again, also because of the interposition

13. Scholiast: "This is also in book 11 of the *On Nature*; for, he says, if its size had been reduced because of the distance, its brightness would have been even more reduced; for there is no other distance more symmetrical with this [degree of brightness]."

14. Scholiast: "But not at the same time."

[of other bodies], and in all the ways which the phenomena in our experience suggest for the explanation of this kind of thing—as long as one is not so enamoured of the method of unique explanations as to groundlessly reject the others, because of a failure to understand what it is possible for a man to understand and what is not, for this reason desiring to understand what cannot be understood. And again, it is possible that the moon produces its own light, and also possible that it receives it from the sun. 95. For in our own experience we see many things which produce their own light, and many which receive it from other things. And none of the meteorological phenomena is a hindrance [to these possibilities], as long as one always remembers the method of several different explanations, considers together the hypotheses and explanations compatible with these, and does not, by looking to things which are not compatible, give them a pointless importance and so slide, in different ways on different occasions, into the method of unique explanations. And the appearance of a face in [the moon] could occur because of the variation among its parts, and because [some parts] are blocked, and by all the methods one might consider which are consistent with the phenomena. 96. For in the case of all the meteorological phenomena one must not give up tracking down such [possibilities]. For if one is in conflict with the clear facts, one will never be able to partake of genuine freedom from disturbance.

The eclipse of the sun and the moon could also come to pass by extinguishing, as is also observed to occur in our experience; and also by being blocked by certain other bodies, either the earth or the heavens or some other such thing. And one should in this way consider the methods [of explanation] which are consistent with each other, and that it is not impossible that some of them may occur together. [15]

97. And again, we should grasp the orderliness of the cyclical periods [of the heavenly bodies] [as happening] in the same way that some of the things which also happen in our experience [occur]; and let the nature of the divine not be brought to bear on this at all, but let it go on being thought of as free from burdensome service and as [living] in complete blessedness. For if this is not done, the entire study of the explanations for meteorological phenomena will be pointless, as it has already been for some who did not pursue the method of possible explanations and so were reduced to pointlessness because they thought that [the phenomena] only occurred in one manner and rejected all the other explanations

---

15. Scholiast: "He says the same in book 12 of *On Nature*, and in addition that the sun is eclipsed by the fact that the moon darkens it, and the moon by the shadow of the earth, but also by its own retreat. This is also said by Diogenes the Epicurean in book 1 of his *Selections*."

which were also possible, and so were swept off into an unintelligible position and were unable to consider together the phenomena which one must accept as signs.

98. The varying lengths of nights and days [could occur] as a result of the alternate swift and slow motions of the sun over the earth, ⟨or even⟩ as a result of covering the varying distances between places and certain places either faster or slower, as is also observed [to happen] with some things in our experience; and we must speak in a manner consistent with these when we speak of meteorological phenomena. But those who accept one explanation are in conflict with the phenomena and have lost track of what it is possible for a man to understand.

Predictive weather signs could occur as a result of coincidental conjunctions of events, as in the case of animals which are evident in our experience, and also as a result of alterations and changes in the air. For both of these are not in conflict with the phenomena; 99. but it is not possible to see in what sort of cases the explanation is given by reference to this or that cause.

Clouds could come to be and to be formed both as a result of thickenings of air caused by the pressure of the winds, and as a result of the entanglements of atoms which grip one another and are suitable for producing this effect, and as a result of a collection of effluences from both earth and bodies of water; and it is not impossible that the formation of such compounds is also produced in several other ways. So rains [lit. waters] could be produced from the clouds, sometimes when they are compressed and sometimes when they undergo change; 100. and again, winds, by their egress from suitable places and motion through the air, [can cause rain] when there is a relatively forceful influx from certain aggregates which are suitable for such discharges.

Thunder can occur as a result of the confinement of wind in the hollows of the clouds, as happens in closed vessels [in] our [experience], and as a result of the booming of fire combined with wind inside the clouds, and as a result of the rupture and separation of clouds, and by the friction between clouds and their fragmentation when they have taken on an ice-like solidity. And the phenomena invite us to say that the entire topic as well as this part of it are subject to several different explanations.

101. And lightning flashes similarly occur in several different ways; for the [atomic] configuration which produces fire is squeezed out by the friction and collision of clouds and so generates a lightning flash; [it could] also [occur] as a result of the wind making the sort of bodies which cause this luminiscence flash forth from the clouds; and by the squeezing of clouds when they are compressed, either by each other or by the winds; and by the inclusion [in them] of the light scattered from

the heavenly bodies, which is then driven together by the motion of the clouds and winds and is expelled by the clouds; or as a result of the filtering of the finest form of light through the clouds[16] and as a result of its movement; and by the conflagration of the wind which occurs because of the vigour of its movement and its extreme compression; **102.** and because the clouds are broken by the winds and the atoms which produce fire are then expelled and so produce the presentation of the lightning flash. And it will be easy to see [that it could happen] in a great many other ways, for him who clings always to the phenomena and who is able to contemplate together what is similar to the phenomena.

The lightning flash precedes the thunder in this sort of arrangement of clouds because the configuration which produces the lightning flash is expelled at the same time as the wind strikes [the cloud] and subsequently the wind, being confined, produces this booming noise; and because although both strike together, the lightning flash moves with a more vigorous speed towards us, **103.** while the thunder comes later, just as happens with some things which strike blows and are observed from a distance.

Thunder bolts can occur as a result of repeated gatherings of winds, and their compression and powerful conflagration, and the fracture of one part and its very powerful expulsion towards the areas below, the breakage occurring because the places adjacent to it are more dense owing to the thickening of the clouds; and [it may occur] just as thunder too can occur, simply because of the expulsion of the fire, when a great deal of it is confined and very powerfully struck by the wind and has broken the cloud because it cannot escape to the adjacent areas since they are always compacting together.[17] **104.** And thunderbolts can be produced in several different ways—just be sure that myths are kept out of it! And they will be kept out of it if one follows rightly the appearances and takes them as signs of what is unobservable.

Whirlwinds can occur as a result of a cloud being forced in the form of a column downwards to regions below, being pushed by a mass of wind and driven by the power of the wind, while at the same time the wind outside pushes the cloud to one side; and by the formation of the wind into a circle when some air presses down on it from above; and as a result of the compacting of the air around it, when a great flow of winds takes place and is not able to flow off to the side. **105.** And when the whirlwind

16. Scholiast: "Or clouds were incinerated by the fire and the thunder is produced."

17. Scholiast: "It generally [strikes] on a high mountain, on which thunder bolts most often fall."

is forced down to the earth, tornadoes are produced, in whatever way their production might take place owing to the movement of the wind; and when it [is forced down] on the sea, waterspouts are produced.

It is possible that earthquakes occur as a result of the enclosure of wind in the earth and the juxtaposition of small masses [of wind?] with the earth and its constant movement, all of which produce the shaking in the earth. And [the earth] either takes this wind into itself from the outside or because solid blocks of earth fall inwards into cavernous places in the earth and turn the enclosed air into wind. ‹And› earthquakes may also be produced as a result of the mere transmission of the movement produced by the falling of many solid blocks of earth and the transmission [of this shock] back again when it collides with some more densely compressed parts of the earth. **106**. And these movements of the earth may also occur in many other ways. [There may be a lacuna in our text here.]

And the winds happen to occur from time to time when on any occasion some foreign matter gradually enters in, and as a result of the collection of a tremendous amount of water; and the rest of the winds occur when even just a few fall into the many hollow spaces, if there occurs a transmission of their force.

Hail is produced by a quite powerful solidification, [a result of] a circular movement and [subsequent] division of certain breathlike particles; and also ‹because of› a more moderate solidification of certain watery particles ‹and› their simultaneous fracture, which at the same time condenses them and breaks them up, so that the solidified material forms compounds both within the distinct parts and in the aggregation. **107**. It is not impossible that their circular shape is produced both because the extremities on all sides melt off and because, at the formation of the compound, [particles] (either watery or breathlike) surround it evenly, part by part on all sides, as is said.

Snow could be produced by the outpouring of fine [drops of] water from the clouds owing to the symmetry of the pores and to the constant and powerful friction on the right sort of clouds by the wind, followed by the solidification of this [water] during its movement as a result of some powerful conditions of coldness in the lower regions of the clouds. And as a result of a solidification in the clouds which have a uniform rareness this sort of outflow can also occur when the watery clouds rub against each other and lie side by side; and these cause a kind of compression and so produce hail—something which happens mostly in the spring. **108**. And this aggregation of snow could also vibrate off when the clouds which have undergone solidification rub against each other. And it is also possible that snow is produced in other ways.

Dew is produced by the assembling from the air of [particles] which become productive of this sort of moisture; and also by an exhalation either from wet areas or areas which have bodies of water (which is the sort of place where dew is most likely to be produced) followed by their assembling in the same place and their production of moisture and finally by its movement to lower regions, exactly as certain such things in our own experience ‹are observed being produced. And frost› **109.** is produced ‹no differently› from dew, when certain such things are solidified in a certain way because of a certain condition of cold air.

Ice is produced both by the expulsion of the round configuration from the water and by the compression of the scalene and acute-angled [particles] which exist in the water; and also by the addition from the outside of such [particles], which are driven together and so produce solidification in the water by expelling a certain number of round [particles].

The rainbow occurs as a result of the sun shining on water-laden air; or as a result of some peculiar coalescence of light and air which will produce the peculiar properties of these colours, either all [together] or one type at a time; and again, as a result of the reflection of this light the neighbouring regions of the air will take on the sort of coloration which we see because the sun shines on its parts. **110.** This presentation of roundness occurs because the vision observes the distance as [being] equal from all directions, or [possibly] because the atoms in the air (or those in the clouds which are derived from the same air) are compressed in such a way that this compound gives off [the appearance of] roundness.

The halo around the moon is produced because air from all sides moves towards the moon; or when it evenly restricts [the movement of] the effluences sent off from it to such an extent that this cloudlike phenomenon forms around it in a circle and is not interrupted in the slightest extent; or it restricts [the movement of] the air around it symmetrically on all sides so that what is around it takes on a round and dense formation. **111.** And this happens in certain parts either because a certain effluence forces its way in from outside or because heat occupies passages suitable for the production of this effect.

Comets occur when, under suitable circumstances, fire is collected in certain places in the meteorological region at certain intervals of time; or when from time to time the heavens above us adopt a particular kind of movement, so that such heavenly bodies make their appearance; or the [comets] just rush in by themselves at certain times because of some circumstances and approach the regions where we happen to be and become prominently visible; and they disappear owing to opposite causes. **112.** Certain heavenly bodies rotate in place [i.e., those near the pole, which never set], which occurs not only because that part of the cosmos around which the rest rotates is stationary, as some people say, but also because there is a circular rotation of air around it which prevents them from wandering around, as the other heavenly bodies do; or also because they do not have any appropriate fuel in adjacent regions, while there is [a supply of fuel] in the area where they are observed. And this [phenomenon] could also be produced in several other ways, provided one can reason out what is consistent with the appearances.

The wandering of some of the heavenly bodies, if they really do happen to have this kind of movement, 113. and the regular motion of others could be a result of them starting out with circular movement and [then] having been forced in such a way that some of them move in the same uniform rotation while others move with a rotation which at the same time has certain irregularities; and it could also be that, according to the regions over which they move, in one place there are uniform regions of air which push them on continuously in the same direction and which burn uniformly, while elsewhere there are irregular [regions of air] of such a nature that the observed differences are produced. But to supply one cause for these facts, when the phenomena suggest that there are several different explanations, is the lunatic and inappropriate behaviour of those who are obsessed with a pointless [brand of] astronomy and of certain [others] who supply vain explanations, since they do not in any way liberate the divine nature from burdensome service. 114. That some heavenly bodies are observed being left behind by others occurs because although they move around in the same orbit they do so more slowly; and because they also move in the opposite direction being drawn backwards by the same rotation; and also because some rotate through a larger area and some through a smaller, though they turn with the same rotation. But to pronounce unqualifiedly on these matters is appropriate to those who wish [only] to make a display of wonders for the masses.

So-called falling stars could be produced in part by their own friction, and also because they fall wherever there is a massive outburst of wind, just as we said [occurred] in the case of lightning flashes; 115. also by a collection of atoms capable of producing fire, when similar material [congregates] to produce this result and also a motion where the surge produced by the original collection occurs; and also because wind is concentrated in certain dense and misty places and this ignites as a result of its confinement, then breaks through the surrounding environment and is borne to the place to which the movement makes its surge; and there are other non-mythical ways in which this phenomenon could be produced.

The predictive weather signs which occur in certain animals occur by a coincidental conjunction of events; for the animals do not bring any necessity to bear on the production of winter, nor does any divine nature sit around waiting for these animals to come out [of hibernation] and [only] then fulfils these signs. **116.** For such foolishness would not afflict any ordinary animal, even if it were a little more sophisticated, let alone one who possessed complete happiness.

Commit all of this to memory, Pythocles; for you will leave myth far behind you and will be able to see [the causes of phenomena] similar to these. Most important, devote yourself to the contemplation of the basic principles [i.e., atoms] and the unlimited [i.e., void] and things related to them, and again [the contemplation] of the criteria and the feelings and the [goal] for sake of which we reason these things out. For if these things above all are contemplated together, they will make it easy for you to see the explanations of the detailed phenomena. For those who have not accepted these [ideas] with complete contentment could not do a good job of contemplating these things themselves, nor could they acquire the [goal] for the sake of which these things should be contemplated.

TEXT 4: *Letter to Menoeceus:* Diogenes Laertius 10.121–135

121. Epicurus to Menoeceus, greetings:

122. Let no one delay the study of philosophy while young nor weary of it when old. For no one is either too young or too old for the health of the soul. He who says either that the time for philosophy has not yet come or that it has passed is like someone who says that the time for happiness has not yet come or that it has passed. Therefore, both young and old must philosophize, the latter so that although old he may stay young in good things owing to gratitude for what has occurred, the former so that although young he too may be like an old man owing to his lack of fear of what is to come. Therefore, one must practise the things which produce happiness, since if that is present we have everything and if it is absent we do everything in order to have it.

123. Do and practise what I constantly told you to do, believing these to be the elements of living well. First, believe that god is an indestructible and blessed animal, in accordance with the general conception of god commonly held, and do not ascribe to god anything foreign to his indestructibility or repugnant to his blessedness. Believe of him everything which is able to preserve his blessedness and indestructibility. For gods do exist, since we have clear knowledge of them. But they are not such as the many believe them to be. For they do not adhere to their own views about the gods. The man who denies the gods of the many is not impious, but rather he who ascribes to the gods the opinions of the many. **124.** For the pronouncements of the many about the gods are not basic grasps but false suppositions. Hence come the greatest harm from the gods to bad men and the greatest benefits [to the good]. For the gods always welcome men who are like themselves, being congenial to their own virtues and considering that whatever is not such is uncongenial.

Get used to believing that death is nothing to us. For all good and bad consists in sense-experience, and death is the privation of sense-experience. Hence, a correct knowledge of the fact that death is nothing to us makes the mortality of life a matter for contentment, not by adding a limitless time [to life] but by removing the longing for immortality. **125.** For there is nothing fearful in life for one who has grasped that there is nothing fearful in the absence of life. Thus, he is a fool who says that he fears death not because it will be painful when present but because it is painful when it is still to come. For that which while present causes no distress causes unnecessary pain when merely anticipated. So death, the most frightening of bad things, is nothing to us; since when we exist, death is not yet present, and when death is present, then we do not exist. Therefore, it is relevant neither to the living nor to the dead, since it does not affect the former, and the latter do not exist. But the many sometimes flee death as the greatest of bad things and sometimes choose it as a relief from the bad things in life. **126.** But the wise man neither rejects life nor fears death. For living does not offend him, nor does he believe not living to be something bad. And just as he does not unconditionally choose the largest amount of food but the most pleasant food, so he savours not the longest time but the most pleasant. He who advises the young man to live well and the old man to die well is simple-minded, not just because of the pleasing aspects of life but because the same kind of practice produces a good life and a good death. Much worse is he who says that it is good not to be born, "but when born to pass through the gates of Hades as quickly as possible."[18] **127.** For if he really believes what he says, why doesn't he leave life? For it is easy for him to do, if he has firmly decided on it. But if he is joking, he is wasting his time among men who don't welcome it. We must remember that what will happen is neither unconditionally within our power nor unconditionally outside our power, so that we will not unconditionally expect that it will occur nor despair of it as unconditionally not going to occur.

One must reckon that of desires some are natural, some groundless; and of the natural desires some are necessary and some merely natural;

18. Theognis 425, 427.

and of the necessary, some are necessary for happiness and some for freeing the body from troubles and some for life itself. **128.** The unwavering contemplation of these enables one to refer every choice and avoidance to the health of the body and the freedom of the soul from disturbance, since this is the goal of a blessed life. For we do everything for the sake of being neither in pain nor in terror. As soon as we achieve this state every storm in the soul is dispelled, since the animal is not in a position to go after some need nor to seek something else to complete the good of the body and the soul. For we are in need of pleasure only when we are in pain because of the absence of pleasure, and when we are not in pain, then we no longer need pleasure.

And this is why we say that pleasure is the starting-point and goal of living blessedly. **129.** For we recognized this as our first innate good, and this is our starting point for every choice and avoidance and we come to this by judging every good by the criterion of feeling. And it is just because this is the first innate good that we do not choose every pleasure; but sometimes we pass up many pleasures when we get a larger amount of what is uncongenial from them. And we believe many pains to be better than pleasures when a greater pleasure follows for a long while if we endure the pains. So every pleasure is a good thing, since it has a nature congenial [to us], but not every one is to be chosen. Just as every pain too is a bad thing, but not every one is such as to be always avoided. **130.** It is, however, appropriate to make all these decisions by comparative measurement and an examination of the advantages and disadvantages. For at some times we treat the good thing as bad and, conversely, the bad thing as good.

And we believe that self-sufficiency is a great good, not in order that we might make do with few things under all circumstances, but so that if we do not have a lot we can make do with few, being genuinely convinced that those who least need extravagance enjoy it most; and that everything natural is easy to obtain and whatever is groundless is hard to obtain; and that simple flavours provide a pleasure equal to that of an extravagant life-style when all pain from want is removed, **131.** and barley cakes and water provide the highest pleasure when someone in want takes them. Therefore, becoming accustomed to simple, not extravagant, ways of life makes one completely healthy, makes man unhesitant in the face of life's necessary duties, puts us in a better condition for the times of extravagance which occasionally come along, and makes us fearless in the face of chance. So when we say that pleasure is the goal we do not mean the pleasures of the profligate or the pleasures of consumption, as some believe, either from ignorance and disagreement or from deliberate misin-

pleasure

terpretation, but rather the lack of pain in the body and disturbance in the soul. **132.** For it is not drinking bouts and continuous partying and enjoying boys and women, or consuming fish and the other dainties of an extravagant table, which produce the pleasant life, but sober calculation which searches out the reasons for every choice and avoidance and drives out the opinions which are the source of the greatest turmoil for men's souls.

Prudence is the principle of all these things and is the greatest good. That is why prudence is a more valuable thing than philosophy. For prudence is the source of all the other virtues, teaching that it is impossible to live pleasantly without living prudently, honourably, and justly, and impossible to live prudently, honourably, and justly without living pleasantly. For the virtues are natural adjuncts of the pleasant life and the pleasant life is inseparable from them.

133. For who do you believe is better than a man who has pious opinions about the gods, is always fearless about death, has reasoned out the natural goal of life and understands that the limit of good things is easy to achieve completely and easy to provide, and that the limit of bad things either has a short duration or causes little trouble?

As to [Fate], introduced by some as the mistress of all, ⟨he is scornful, saying rather that some things happen of necessity,⟩ others by chance, and others by our own agency, and that he sees that necessity is not answerable [to anyone], that chance is unstable, while what occurs by our own agency is autonomous, and that it is to this that praise and blame are attached. **134.** For it would be better to follow the stories told about the gods than to be a slave to the fate of the natural philosophers. For the former suggests a hope of escaping bad things by honouring the gods, but the latter involves an inescapable and merciless necessity. And he [the wise man] believes that chance is not a god, as the many think, for nothing is done in a disorderly way by god; nor that it is an uncertain cause. For he does not think that anything good or bad with respect to living blessedly is given by chance to men, although it does provide the starting points of great good and bad things. And he thinks it better to be unlucky in a rational way than lucky in a senseless way; **135.** for it is better for a good decision not to turn out right in action than for a bad decision to turn out right because of chance.

Practise these and the related precepts day and night, by yourself and with a like-minded friend, and you will never be disturbed either when awake or in sleep, and you will live as a god among men. For a man who lives among immortal goods is in no respect like a mere mortal animal.

Ancient collections of maxims

TEXT 5: *The Principal Doctrines:* Diogenes Laertius 10.139–154

I What is blessed and indestructible has no troubles itself, nor does it give trouble to anyone else, so that it is not affected by feelings of anger or gratitude. For all such things are a sign of weakness.[19]

II Death is nothing to us. For what has been dissolved has no sense-experience, and what has no sense-experience is nothing to us.

III The removal of all feeling of pain is the limit of the magnitude of pleasures. Wherever a pleasurable feeling is present, for as long as it is present, there is neither a feeling of pain nor a feeling of distress, nor both together.

IV The feeling of pain does not linger continuously in the flesh; rather, the sharpest is present for the shortest time, while what merely exceeds the feeling of pleasure in the flesh lasts only a few days. And diseases which last a long time involve feelings of pleasure which exceed feelings of pain.

V It is impossible to live pleasantly without living prudently, honourably, and justly and impossible to live prudently, honourably, and justly without living pleasantly. And whoever lacks this cannot live pleasantly.

VI The natural good of public office and kingship is for the sake of getting confidence from [other] men, [at least] from those from whom one *is* able to provide this.

VII Some men want to become famous and respected, believing that this is the way to acquire security against [other] men. Thus if the life of such men is secure, they acquire the natural good; but if it is not secure, they do not have that for the sake of which they strove from the beginning according to what is naturally congenial.

VIII No pleasure is a bad thing in itself. But the things which produce certain pleasures bring troubles many times greater than the pleasures.

19. Scholiast: "Elsewhere he says that the gods are contemplated by reason, and that some exist 'numerically' [i.e., are numerically distinct, each being unique in kind] while others are similar in form, because of a continuous flow of similar images to the same place; and that they are anthropomorphic."

IX If every pleasure were condensed and were present, both in time and in the whole compound [body and soul] or in the most important parts of our nature, then pleasures would never differ from one another.

X If the things which produce the pleasures of profligate men dissolved the intellect's fears about the phenomena of the heavens and about death and pains and, moreover, if they taught us the limit of our desires, then we would not have reason to criticize them, since they would be filled with pleasures from every source and would contain no feeling of pain or distress from any source—and that is what is bad.

XI If our suspicions about heavenly phenomena and about death did not trouble us at all and were never anything to us, and, moreover, if not knowing the limits of pains and desires did not trouble us, then we would have no need of natural science.

XII It is impossible for someone ignorant about the nature of the universe but still suspicious about the subjects of the myths to dissolve his feelings of fear about the most important matters. So it is impossible to receive unmixed pleasures without knowing natural science.

XIII It is useless to obtain security from men while the things above and below the earth and, generally, the things in the unbounded remained as objects of suspicion.

XIV The purest security is that which comes from a quiet life and withdrawal from the many, although a certain degree of security from other men does come by means of the power to repel [attacks] and by means of prosperity.

XV Natural wealth is both limited and easy to acquire. But wealth [as defined by] groundless opinions extends without limit.

XVI Chance has a small impact on the wise man, while reasoning has arranged for, is arranging for, and will arrange for the greatest and most important matters throughout the whole of his life.

XVII The just life is most free from disturbance, but the unjust life is full of the greatest disturbance.

XVIII As soon as the feeling of pain produced by want is removed, pleasure in the flesh will not increase but is only varied. But the limit of mental pleasures is produced by a reasoning out of these very pleasures [of the flesh] and of the things related to these, which used to cause the greatest fears in the intellect.

XIX Unlimited time and limited time contain equal [amounts of] pleasure, if one measures its limits by reasoning.

XX The flesh took the limits of pleasure to be unlimited, and [only] an unlimited time would have provided it. But the intellect, reasoning out the goal and limit of the flesh and dissolving the fears of eternity, provided us with the perfect way of life and had no further need of unlimited time. But it [the intellect] did not flee pleasure, and even when circumstances caused an exit from life it did not die as though it were lacking any aspect of the best life.

XXI He who has learned the limits of life knows that it is easy to provide that which removes the feeling of pain owing to want and make one's whole life perfect. So there is no need for things which involve struggle.

XXII One must reason about the real goal and every clear fact, to which we refer mere opinions. If not, everything will be full of indecision and disturbance.

XXIII If you quarrel with all your sense-perceptions you will have nothing to refer to in judging even those sense-perceptions which you claim are false.

XXIV If you reject unqualifiedly any sense-perception and do not distinguish the opinion about what awaits confirmation, and what is already present in the sense-perception, and the feelings, and every application of the intellect to presentations, you will also disturb the rest of your sense-perceptions with your pointless opinion; as a result you will reject every criterion. If, on the other hand, in your conceptions formed by opinion, you affirm everything that awaits confirmation as well as what does not, you will not avoid falsehood, so that you will be in the position of maintaining every disputable point in every decision about what is and is not correct.

XXV If you do not, on every occasion, refer each of your actions to the goal of nature, but instead turn prematurely to some other [criterion] in avoiding or pursuing [things], your actions will not be consistent with your reasoning.

XXVI The desires which do not bring a feeling of pain when not fulfilled are not necessary; but the desire for them is easy to dispel when they seem to be hard to achieve or to produce harm.

XXVII Of the things which wisdom provides for the blessedness of one's whole life, by far the greatest is the possession of friendship.

XXVIII The same understanding produces confidence about there being nothing terrible which is eternal or [even] long-lasting and has also realized that security amid even these limited [bad things] is most easily achieved through friendship.

XXIX Of desires, some are natural and necessary, some natural and not necessary, and some neither natural nor necessary but occurring as a result of a groundless opinion.[20]

20. Scholiast: "Epicurus thinks that those which liberate us from pains are natural and necessary, for example drinking in the case of thirst; natural and not

XXX Among natural desires, those which do not lead to a feeling of pain if not fulfilled and about which there is an intense effort, these are produced by a groundless opinion and they fail to be dissolved not because of their own nature but because of the groundless opinions of mankind.

XXXI The justice of nature is a pledge of reciprocal usefulness, [i.e.,] neither to harm one another nor be harmed.

XXXII There was no justice or injustice with respect to all those animals which were unable to make pacts about neither harming one another nor being harmed. Similarly, [there was no justice or injustice] for all those nations which were unable or unwilling to make pacts about neither harming one another nor being harmed.

XXXIII Justice was not a thing in its own right, but [exists] in mutual dealings in whatever places there [is] a pact about neither harming one another nor being harmed.

XXXIV Injustice is not a bad thing in its own right, but [only] because of the fear produced by the suspicion that one will not escape the notice of those assigned to punish such actions.

XXXV It is impossible for someone who secretly does something which men agreed [not to do] in order to avoid harming one another or being harmed to be confident that he will escape detection, even if in current circumstances he escapes detection ten thousand times. For until his death it will be uncertain whether he will continue to escape detection.

XXXVI In general outline justice is the same for everyone; for it was something useful in mutual associations. But with respect to the peculiarities of a region or of other [relevant] causes, it does not follow that the same thing is just for everyone.

XXXVII Of actions believed to be just, that whose usefulness in circumstances of mutual associations is supported by the testimony [of experience] has the attribute of serving as just whether it is the same for everyone or not. And if someone passes a law and it does not turn out to be in accord with what is useful in mutual associations, this no longer possesses the nature of justice. And if what is useful in the sense of being just changes, but for a while fits our basic grasp [of justice], nevertheless it was just for that length of time, [at least] for those who do not disturb themselves with empty words but simply look to the facts.

---

necessary are those which merely provide variations of pleasure but do not remove the feeling of pain, for example expensive foods; neither natural nor necessary are, for example, crowns and the erection of statues."

XXXVIII If objective circumstances have not changed and things believed to be just have been shown in actual practice not to be in accord with our basic grasp [of justice], then those things were not just. And if objective circumstances do change and the same things which had been just turn out to be no longer useful, then those things were just as long as they were useful for the mutual associations of fellow citizens; but later, when they were not useful, they were no longer just.

XXXIX The man who has made the best arrangements for confidence about external threats is he who has made the manageable things akin to himself, and has at least made the unmanageable things not alien to himself. But he avoided all contact with things for which not even this could be managed and he drove out of his life everything which it profited him to drive out.

XL All those who had the power to acquire the greatest confidence from [the threats posed by] their neighbours also thereby lived together most pleasantly with the surest guarantee; and since they enjoyed the fullest sense of belonging they did not grieve the early death of the departed, as though it called for pity.

TEXT 6: *The Vatican Collection of Epicurean Sayings*[21]

4. Every pain is easy to despise. For [pains] which produce great distress are short in duration; and those which last for a long time in the flesh cause only mild distress.

7. It is hard to commit injustice and escape detection, but to be confident of escaping detection is impossible.

9. Necessity is a bad thing, but there is no necessity to live with necessity.

11. In most men, what is at peace is numbed and what is active is raging madly.

14. We are born only once, and we cannot be born twice; and one must for all eternity exist no more. You are not in control of tomorrow and yet you delay your [opportunity to] rejoice. Life is ruined by delay and each and every one of us dies without enjoying leisure.

15. We value our characters as our own personal possessions, whether they are good and envied by men or not. We must regard our neighbours' characters thus too, if they are respectable.

21. Some of the maxims in this collection are identical to some Principal Doctrines; some are attributed to Epicurus' followers rather than to the master himself. The Sayings selected by Arrighetti (in *Epicuro: Opere*) are translated here and his text is used.

16. No one who sees what is bad chooses it, but being lured [by it] as being good compared to what is even worse than it he is caught in the snare.

17. It is not the young man who is to be congratulated for his blessedness, but the old man who has lived well. For the young man at the full peak of his powers wanders senselessly, owing to chance. But the old man has let down anchor in old age as though in a harbour, since he has secured the goods about which he was previously not confident by means of his secure sense of gratitude.

18. If you take away the chance to see and talk and spend time with [the beloved], then the passion of sexual love is dissolved.

19. He who forgets the good which he previously had, has today become an old man.

21. One must not force nature but persuade her. And we will persuade her by fulfilling the necessary desires, and the natural ones too if they do not harm [us], but sharply rejecting the harmful ones.

23. Every friendship is worth choosing[22] for its own sake, though it takes its origin from the benefits [it confers on us].

24. Dreams have neither a divine nature, nor prophetic power, but they are produced by the impact of images.

25. Poverty, if measured by the goal of nature, is great wealth; and wealth, if limits are not set for it, is great poverty.

26. One must grasp clearly that both long and short discourses contribute to the same [end].

27. In other activities, the rewards come only when people have become, with great difficulty, complete [masters of the activity]; but in philosophy the pleasure accompanies the knowledge. For the enjoyment does not come after the learning but the learning and the enjoyment are simultaneous.

28. One must not approve of those who are excessively eager for friendship, nor those who are reluctant. But one must be willing to run some risks for the sake of friendship.

29. Employing frankness in my study of natural philosophy, I would prefer to proclaim in oracular fashion what is beneficial to men, even if no one is going to understand, rather than to assent to [common] opinions and so enjoy the constant praise which comes from the many.

31. (= Metrodorus fr. 51) One can attain security against other things, but when it comes to death all men live in a city without walls.

22. This is an emendation for the mss' 'a virtue'; we regard the emendation as virtually certain, though the transmitted text has been defended.

32. To show reverence for a wise man is itself a great good for him who reveres [the wise man].

33. The cry of the flesh: not to be hungry, not to be thirsty, not to be cold. For if someone has these things and is confident of having them in the future, he might contend even with ⟨Zeus⟩ for happiness.

34. We do not need utility from our friends so much as we need confidence concerning that utility.

35. One should not spoil what is present by desiring what is absent, but rather reason out that these things too [i.e., what we have] were among those we might have prayed for.

37. Nature is weak in the face of the bad, not the good; for it is preserved by pleasures and dissolved by pains.

38. He is utterly small-minded for whom there are many plausible reasons for committing suicide.

39. The constant friend is neither he who always searches for utility, nor he who never links [friendship to utility]. For the former makes gratitude a matter for commercial transaction, while the latter kills off good hope for the future.

40. He who claims that everything occurs by necessity has no complaint against him who claims that everything does not occur by necessity. For he makes the very claim [in question] by necessity.

41. One must philosophize and at the same time laugh and take care of one's household and use the rest of our personal goods, and never stop proclaiming the utterances of correct philosophy.

42. In the same period of time both the greatest good and the dissolution ⟨of bad⟩ are produced.

43. It is impious to love money unjustly, and shameful to do so justly; for it is unfitting to be sordidly stingy even if one is just.

44. When the wise man is brought face to face with the necessities of life, he knows how to give rather than receive—such a treasury of self-sufficiency has he found.

45. Natural philosophy does not create boastful men nor chatterboxes nor men who show off the 'culture' which the many quarrel over, but rather strong and self-sufficient men, who pride themselves on their own personal goods, not those of external circumstances.

46. We utterly eliminate bad habits like wicked men who have been doing great harm to us for a long time.

48. [We should] try to make the later stretch of the road more important than the earlier one, as long as we are on the road; and when we get to the end [of the road], [we should] feel a smooth contentment.

52. Friendship dances around the world announcing to all of us that we must wake up to blessedness.

53. One should envy no one. For the good are not worthy of envy, and the more good fortune the wicked have, the more they spoil it for themselves.

54. One must not pretend to philosophize, but philosophize in reality. For we do not need the semblance of health but true health.

55. Misfortunes must be cured by a sense of gratitude for what has been and the knowledge that what is past cannot be undone.

56–57. The wise man feels no more pain when he is tortured ‹than when his friend is tortured, and will die on his behalf; for if he betrays› his friend, his entire life will be confounded and utterly upset because of a lack of confidence.

58. They must free themselves from the prison of general education and politics.

59. The stomach is not insatiable, as the many say, but rather the opinion that the stomach requires an unlimited amount of filling is false.

60. Everyone leaves life as though he had just been born.

61. The sight of one's neighbours is most beautiful if the first meeting brings concord or [at least] produces a serious commitment to this.

62. For if parents are justifiably angered at their children, it is surely pointless to resist and not ask to be forgiven; but if [their anger] is not justifiable but somewhat irrational, it is ridiculous for someone with irrationality in his heart to appeal to someone set against appeals and not to seek in a spirit of good will to win him over by other means.

63. There is also a proper measure for parsimony, and he who does not reason it out is just as badly off as he who goes wrong by total neglect of limits.

64. Praise from other men must come of its own accord; and we must be concerned with healing ourselves.

65. It is pointless to ask from the gods what one is fully able to supply for oneself.

66. Let us share our friends' suffering not with laments but with thoughtful concern.

67. A free life cannot acquire great wealth, because the task is not easy without slavery to the mob or those in power; rather, it already possesses everything in constant abundance. And if it does somehow achieve great wealth, one could easily share this out in order to obtain the good will of one's neighbours.

68. Nothing is enough to someone for whom enough is little.

69. The ingratitude of the soul makes an animal greedy for unlimited variation in its life-style.

70. Let nothing be done in your life which will cause you to fear if it is discovered by your neighbour.

71. One should bring this question to bear on all one's desires: what will happen to me if what is sought by desire is achieved, and what will happen if it is not?

73. Even some bodily pains are worthwhile for fending off others like them.

74. In a joint philosophical investigation he who is defeated comes out ahead in so far as he has learned something new.

75. This utterance is ungrateful for past goods: look to the end of a long life.

76. As you grow old, you are such as I would praise, and you have seen the difference between what it means to philosophize for yourself and what it means to do so for Greece. I rejoice with you.

77. The greatest fruit of self-sufficiency is freedom.

78. The noble man is most involved with wisdom and friendship, of which one is a mortal good, the other immortal.

79. He who is free from disturbance within himself also causes no trouble for another.

80. A young man's share in salvation comes from attending to his age and guarding against what will defile everything through maddening desires.

81. The disturbance of the soul will not be dissolved nor will considerable joy be produced by the presence of the greatest wealth, nor by honour and admiration among the many, nor by anything which is a result of indefinite causes.

Doxographical reports

TEXT 7: *Introductory report of his views:* Diogenes Laertius 10.29–34

29. . . . So philosophy is divided into three parts: canonic, physics, ethics. **30.** Canonic provides procedures for use in the system and it is contained in one work entitled *The Canon*. Physics comprises the entire study of nature and it is contained in the 37 books of the *On Nature* and in outline form in the letters. Ethics comprises the discussion of choice and avoidance and it is contained in the book *On Ways of Life* and in the letters and in *On the Goal of Life*. They are accustomed, however, to set out canonic together with physics and they describe it as dealing with the criterion and with the basic principle, and as being fundamental. And physics is about generation and destruction, and about nature. And ethics is about things worth choosing and avoiding and about ways of life and about the goal of life.

31. They reject dialectic as being irrelevant. For it is sufficient for natural philosophers to proceed according to the utterances made by the facts. So, in *The Canon* Epicurus is found saying that sense-perceptions, basic grasps, and feelings are the criteria of truth, and the Epicureans add the applications of the intellect to presentations. He says this also in the epitome addressed to Herodotus and in the *Principal Doctrines*. "For," he says, "every sense-perception is unreasoning and incapable of remembering. For neither is it moved by itself nor can it add or subtract anything when moved by something else. Nor is there anything which can refute sense-perceptions. **32.** For a perception from one sense cannot refute another of the same type, because they are of equal strength; nor can a perception from one sense refute one from a different sense, because they do not judge the same objects. Nor indeed can reasoning [refute them]; for all reasoning depends on the sense-perceptions. Nor can one sense-perception refute another, since we attend to them all. And the fact of our awareness of sense-perceptions confirms the truth of the sense-perceptions. And it is just as much a fact that we see and hear as that we feel pain; hence, it is from the apparent that we must infer about the non-evident. Moreover, all ideas are formed from sense-perceptions by direct experience or by analogy or by similarity or by compounding, with reasoning also making a contribution. And the appear-

41

ances which madmen have and those in dreams are true, for they cause motion [in minds], and what does not exist does not move anything."

33. They say that the basic grasp is like an act of grasping or a correct opinion or a conception or a universal idea stored [up in the mind], i.e., a memory of what has often appeared in the external world. For example, this sort of thing is "man". For as soon as "man" is uttered, immediately one has an idea of the general outline of man, according to our basic grasp, following the lead of our senses. Therefore, what is primarily denoted by every word is something clear; and we could never have inquired into an object if we had not first been aware of it. For example, "is what is standing far off a horse or a cow?" For one must at some time have been aware of the shape of horse and cow according to a basic grasp.

Nor would we have given a name to something if we had not first learned its general outline according to a basic grasp. Therefore, our basic grasps are clear. And an object of opinion depends on something prior and clear, by referring to which we speak [of it], for example, "On what basis do we know if this is a man?"

34. And they also say that opinion is a supposition, and that it can be true or false. For if it is testified for or not testified against, it is true. But if it is not testified for or is testified against, it turns out false. Hence they introduced the idea of "what awaits confirmation." For example, one awaits confirmation of and comes nearer to a tower, to learn how it appears close up.

They say there are two feelings, pleasure and pain, which occur in every animal; and the one is congenial to us, the other uncongenial. By means of them we judge what to choose and what to avoid. Of inquiries, some deal with objective facts, others with mere words.

This, then, is an elementary account of the division of philosophy and the criterion.

TEXT 8: *Report of Epicurus' Ethical Views:* Diogenes Laertius
              10.117–121

117. . . . He writes as follows on matters related to living and how we should choose some things and avoid others. But first let us relate the opinions of Epicurus and his followers about the wise man.

Harm from other men comes either as a result of hate or envy or contempt, which the wise man overcomes by reasoning. Moreover, once a man has become wise he can no longer take on the opposite disposition nor feign it willingly. But he will be more affected by feelings—for they would not hinder his progress towards wisdom. Nor indeed could people with every bodily condition become wise, nor can people from every race. **118.** And even if the wise man is tortured on the rack, he is happy. Only the wise man will be grateful and he will persist in speaking well of friends equally whether they are present or absent. But when he is tortured on the rack he will moan and groan. The wise man will not have intercourse with a woman in a manner forbidden by the laws, according to Diogenes in his summary of Epicurus' ethical doctrines. Nor will he punish his servants, but rather will pity them and forgive one who is virtuous. They do not believe that the wise man will fall in love, nor that he will worry about his burial, nor that love is sent by the gods, according to Diogenes in his . . . [There is a lacuna here.] . . . Nor will he be a good public speaker. "Sexual intercourse", they say, "never helped anyone, and one must be satisfied if it has not harmed."

119. And indeed the wise man will marry and father children, as Epicurus says in his *Problems* and in the *On Nature*. But he will marry [only] when it is indicated by the circumstances of his life at a given time. And some will be diverted from this. Nor indeed will he rant and rave while under the influence of drink, as Epicurus says in his *Symposium*. Nor will he participate in civic life, as he says in book one of *On Ways of Life*. Neither will he be a tyrant or a Cynic, as he says in book two of *On Ways of Life*; nor will he be a beggar. But if he were to be blinded he would go on living, as he says in the same book. And the wise man will feel pain, as Diogenes says in book five of his *Selections*. **120a.** And he will serve as a juror, and leave written treatises, though he will not deliver panegyrics. And he will take thought for his possessions and for the future. He will like the countryside. He will resist fate, and will betray none of his friends. He will take thought for good reputation only so far as [to ensure] that he is not held in contempt. He will take more delight in contemplation than other men.

121b. He will erect statues. If he is ⟨well⟩ off, he will be indifferent to it. Only the wise man could converse properly on music and poetry, but he will not actually write poems. One [wise man] is no wiser than another. He will earn money when in dire straits, but only by [exploiting] his wisdom. And he will serve a monarch, when the occasion is appropriate. He will be grateful to someone for being corrected. And he will set up a school, but not so as to draw a crowd. And he will give a public reading, but not unless pressed. He will hold firm opinions and will not be at a loss. And he will be of the same character while asleep. And he will sometimes die for a friend.

120b. They believe that [moral] errors are not equal. And that health is for some a good thing and for others an indifferent. Courage does not come to be by nature, but by a reasoning out of what is advantageous.

And friendship comes to be because of its utility; but one must neverthe-less make a preliminary sacrifice [for a friend] (for one must also sow the ground), and it is [then] formed by a sharing among those who are ful-filled by their pleasures.

121a. Happiness is conceived of in two ways: the highest happiness, which is that of god and does not admit of further intensification, and that which ⟨is determined by⟩ the addition and subtraction of pleasures.

TEXT 9: Diogenes Laertius 10.136–138

136. He disagrees with the Cyrenaics on the question of pleasure. For they do not admit katastematic pleasure, but only kinetic pleasure, and he admits both types in both the body and the soul, as he says in *On Choice and Avoidance* and in *On the Goal* and in book one of *On Ways of Life* and in the *Letter to His Friends in Mytilene*. Similarly, Diogenes too in book seventeen of his *Selections* and Metrodorus in the *Timocrates* take the same position: both kinetic and katastematic pleasures are conceived of as pleasure. And Epicurus, in his *On Choices*, says this: "For freedom from disturbance and freedom from suffering are katastematic pleasures; and joy and delight are viewed as kinetic and active."

137. Further, he disagrees with the Cyrenaics [thus]. For they think that bodily pains are worse than those of the soul, since people who err are punished with bodily [pain], while he thinks that pains of the soul are worse, since the flesh is only troubled by the present, but the soul is troubled by the past and the present and the future. In the same way, then, the soul also has greater pleasures. And he uses as a proof that the goal is pleasure the fact that animals, as soon as they are born are satis-fied with it but are in conflict with suffering by nature and apart from reason. So it is by our experience all on its own that we avoid pain. . . .

138. The virtues too are chosen because of pleasure, and not for their own sakes, just as medicine is chosen because of health, as Diogenes too says in book twenty of the *Selections*; he also says that basic education is a [form of] pastime. And Epicurus says that only virtue is inseparable from pleasure, and that the other things, such as food, may be separated [from pleasure].

TEXT 10: Diogenes Laertius 2.88–90 (an account of Cyrenaic hedonism)

88. Particular pleasure is worth choosing for its own sake; happiness, however, is not worth choosing for its own sake but because of the par-ticular pleasures. A confirmation that the goal is pleasure is found in the

fact that from childhood on we involuntarily find it [i.e., pleasure] congenial and that when we get it we seek nothing more and that we flee nothing so much as its opposite, pain. And pleasure is good even if it comes
from the most indecorous sources, as Hippobotus says in his *On Choices*.
For even if the deed is out of place, the pleasure at any rate is worth
choosing for its own sake and good.

89. They hold that the removal of the feeling of pain is not pleasure,
as Epicurus said it was, and that absence of pleasure is not pain. For
both are kinetic, while neither absence of pain nor absence of pleasure is
a motion, since absence of pain is like the condition [*katastasis*] of some-
body who is asleep. They say that it is possible that some people do not
choose pleasure, because they are corrupted. However, not all pleasures
and pains of the soul occur as a result of bodily pleasures and pains; for
joy results from the simple prosperity of one's fatherland, just as it does
from one's own. But further, they say, pleasure is not produced by the
recollection or expectation of good things, as Epicurus thought. For the
soul's movement is dissolved by the passage of time. **90.** They say that
pleasures are not produced by the simple act of vision or hearing. At any
rate we enjoy hearing those who imitate lamentations and do not enjoy
hearing genuine lamentations. [They held that] absence of pleasure and
absence of pain are intermediate conditions [*katastaseis*], and moreover
that bodily pleasures are much better than those of the soul, and that
bodily disturbances are worse. And that is why wrong-doers are punished with these instead [of those]. For they supposed that being in pain
is more difficult and that enjoying pleasure is more congenial. . . .

TEXT 11: Clement of Alexandria *Stromates* 2.21,127.2 p. 182 Stählin
               (450 U)

For the Cyrenaics and Epicurus belong to the class of those who take
their starting point from pleasure; for they say expressly that living pleasantly is the goal and that only pleasure is the perfect good, but Epicurus
says that the removal of pain is also pleasure; and he says that that which
first and by itself draws [us] to itself is worth choosing, and obviously this
thing is certainly kinetic.

TEXT 12: *Ibid.* 2.21,128.1, p. 182 Stählin (509 U)

Epicurus and the Cyrenaics say that what is primarily [or: at first] congenial to us is pleasure; for virtue comes along for the sake of pleasure
and produces pleasure.

TEXT 13: *Ibid.* 2.21,130.8–9 pp. 184–5 Stählin (451 U)

. . . These Cyrenaics reject Epicurus' definition of pleasure, i.e., the removal of what causes pain, stigmatizing it as the condition of a corpse; for we rejoice not only over pleasures, but also over conversations and ambitions. But Epicurus thinks that all joy of the soul supervenes on the prior experiences of the body.

The testimony of Cicero

The Roman statesman and philosophical writer, Cicero (active in the first century B.C.), was a lively critic of Epicureanism. He is sometimes unfair and dismissive, but even his polemic yields information of value to the student of Epicureanism.

TEXT 14: *On Goals* 1.18–20

18. Epicurus generally does not go far wrong when he follows Democritus . . . but these are the catastrophes which belong to Epicurus alone. He thinks that these same indivisible and solid bodies move down in a straight line by their own weight and that this is the natural motion of all bodies. 19. Then this clever fellow, when it occurred to him that if they all moved directly down and, as I said, in a straight line, it would never come about that one atom could make contact with another and so . . . he introduced a fictitious notion: he said that an atom swerves by a very little bit, indeed a minimal distance, and that in this way are produced the mutual entanglements, linkages, and cohesions of the atoms as a result of which the world and all the parts of the world and everything in it are produced. . . . The swerve itself is made up to suit his pleasure—for he says that the atom swerves without a cause . . . —and without a cause he tore from the atoms that straight downward motion which is natural to all heavy objects (as he himself declared); and by so doing he did not even achieve the goal he intended when he made up this fiction. 20. For if all the atoms swerve, none will ever cohere in a compound; but if some swerve and some move properly by their own impetus, this will amount, first of all, to assigning different spheres of influence, so to speak, to the atoms, some to move straight, others to move crookedly; and second, that very same confused concourse of atoms (and this is the point which Democritus too had trouble with) will not be able to produce the orderly beauty of this world.

TEXT 15: *On Fate* 18–48 (selections)

18. If it were stated thus, "Scipio will die by violence at night in his room", that would be a true statement. For it would be a statement that what was going to occur actually was going to occur; and one ought to know that it was going to occur from the fact that it did happen. And

"Scipio will die" was no more true than "he will die in that manner", nor was it any more necessary that he die than that he die in that manner; nor was [the statement that] "Scipio was killed" any more immune from a change from truth to falsehood than [the statement that] "Scipio will be killed".

And the fact that these things are so does not mean that Epicurus has any reason to fear fate and seek aid from the atoms by making them swerve from their paths, and so at one time to burden himself with two unsolvable difficulties: first, that something should occur without a cause, which means that something comes to be from nothing (and neither he nor any other physicist believes that); second, that when two atoms move through the void one goes in a straight line and the other swerves.

19. Epicurus can concede that every proposition is either true or false and still not fear that it is necessary that everything occur by fate. For it is not in virtue of eternal causes derived from a necessity of nature that the following proposition is true: "Carneades will go down to the Academy"; but neither is it uncaused. Rather, there is a difference between causes which just happen to precede [the event] and causes which contain in themselves a natural efficacy. So it always was true that "Epicurus will die at the age of seventy-two in the archonship of Pytharatus", but there were not any fated causes why it should occur like this; rather, what happened certainly was going to happen as it [indeed did] happen. 20. And those who say that what is going to occur is immutable and that a true future statement cannot be converted into a false one are not in fact asserting the necessity of fate, but merely indicating what our words mean. But those who introduce an eternal series of causes are the ones who strip the human mind of free will and bind it by the necessity of fate.

But so much for this; let us move on. Chrysippus reasons thus. "If there is a motion without a cause, not every proposition, which the dialecticians call an *axioma*, will be either true or false. For what will not have effective causes will be neither true nor false. But every proposition is either true or false. Therefore, there is no motion without a cause. 21. And if this is so, everything which happens happens in virtue of prior causes; and if this is so, all things happen by fate. So it is shown that whatever happens happens by fate."

First of all, if I here chose to agree with Epicurus and deny that every proposition is either true or false, I would rather accept that blow than approve of the claim that all things happen by fate. For that claim is at least subject to debate, but this latter is intolerable. And so Chrysippus exerts all his efforts to persuade us that every *axioma* is either true or false. Just as Epicurus fears that if he should concede this, he must concede that whatever happens happens by fate (for if one of the two is true from eternity, it is also certain, and if certain, then necessary too: that is how he thinks that necessity and fate are confirmed), so Chrysippus feared that, if he did not maintain that every proposition was either true or false, he could not maintain that everything happened by fate and as a result of eternal causes of future events.

22. But Epicurus thinks that the necessity of fate can be avoided by the swerve of an atom. And so a third kind of motion appears, in addition to weight and collision, when an atom swerves by a minimal interval (he calls it an *elachiston* [smallest]); and he is forced to concede, in fact if not in his words, that this swerve is uncaused. For an atom does not swerve because it is struck by another atom. For how can one be struck by another if the atomic bodies are moving, owing to their weight, downward in straight lines, as Epicurus thinks? It follows that, if one atom is never displaced by another, then one atom cannot even contact another. 23. From which it is also concluded that if an atom exists and it does swerve, it does so without cause. Epicurus introduced this line of reasoning because he was afraid that if an atom always moved by its natural and necessary heaviness, we would have no freedom, since our mind would be moved in such a way that it would be compelled by the motion of atoms. Democritus, the founder of atomism, preferred to accept that all things happened by necessity than to tear from the atomic bodies their natural motions.

Carneades was even more acute and showed that the Epicureans could defend their case without this fictitious swerve. For since they taught that there could be a voluntary motion of the mind, it was better to defend that claim than to introduce the swerve, especially since they could not find a cause for it. And if they defended this [the possibility of a voluntary motion of the mind] they could easily resist Chrysippus' attack. For although they conceded that there was no motion without a cause, they did not concede that everything which occurred occurred by antecedent causes. For there are no external and antecedent causes for our will. 24. Thus we [merely] exploit the common linguistic convention when we say that someone wills or does not will something without cause. For we say "without cause" in order to indicate "without external and antecedent cause," not "without any cause at all"; just as when we refer to an "empty jar" we do not speak as the physicists do, who do not believe that there is a genuinely empty space, but to indicate that the jar is without water or wine or oil, for example. Thus when we say that the mind is moved without cause, we say that it is moved without an external and antecedent cause, not without any cause at all. It can even be said of the atom itself that it moves without a cause when it moves through the void because of weight and heaviness, since there is no external cause.

25. But again, to avoid being mocked by the physicists if we say that anything occurs without a cause, one must make a distinction and say that the nature of the atom itself is such that it moves because of weight and heaviness and that exactly this is the cause of its moving the way it does. Similarly, no external cause is needed for the voluntary motions of the mind; for voluntary motion itself contains within it a nature such that it is in our power and obeys us, but not without a cause. Its very nature is the cause of this fact.

37. ... But from all eternity this proposition was true: "Philoctetes will be abandoned on the island", and this was not able to change from being true to being false. For it is necessary, when you have two contradictories—and here I call contradictories statements one of which affirms something and the other of which denies it—of these, then, it is necessary that one be true and the other false, though Epicurus disagrees. For example, "Philoctetes will be wounded" was true during all previous ages, and "he will not be wounded" was false. Unless, perhaps, we want to accept the view of the Epicureans, who say that such propositions are neither true nor false, or, since they are ashamed of that, say what is [in fact] even more outrageous: that disjunctions of such contradictories are true, but that neither of the propositions contained in them is true. **38.** What an amazing audacity and what a wretched ignorance of logic! For if in speech there is something which is neither true nor false, certainly it is not true. But how can what is not true not be false? Or how can what is not false not be true? So the principle defended by Chrysippus will be retained, that every proposition is either true or false. Reason itself will require that certain things be true from all eternity, that they not have been bound by eternal causes, and that they be free from the necessity of fate. ...

46. This is how this matter should be discussed, rather than seeking help from wandering atoms which swerve from their [natural] course. He says, "an atom swerves." First of all, why? Democritus had already given them another kind of force, that of collision, which he called a "blow"; and you, Epicurus, had given them the force of heaviness and weight. What new cause, then, is there in nature which would make the atom swerve? Or surely you don't mean that they draw lots with each other to see which ones will swerve and which not? Or why do they swerve by the minimal interval, and not by a larger amount? Or why do they swerve by one minimal interval, and not by two or three? This is wishful thinking, not argument. **47.** For you do not say that the atom moves from its place and swerves because it is struck from outside, nor that there is in the void through which the atom moves any trace of a cause for it not to move in a straight line, nor is there any change in the atom itself which would cause it not to maintain the natural motion of its weight. So, although he adduced no cause to produce that swerve, he still thinks that he is making sense when he makes the claim which everyone's mind rejects and recoils from. **48.** And I do not think that there is anyone who does more to confirm, not just fate, but even a powerful necessity governing all things, or who has more effectively abolished voluntary motions of the mind, than [Epicurus], who concedes that he could not have resisted fate in any other way than by taking refuge in these fictitious swerves. For even supposing that there were atoms, which can in no way be proven to my satisfaction, nevertheless, those swerves will remain unexplained. For if it is by natural necessity that atoms move [downwards] owing to their weight, since it is necessary that every heavy body should move and be carried along when there is nothing to prevent it, then it is also necessary for certain atoms (or, if they prefer, all atoms) to swerve, . . . naturally . . .

TEXT 16: *On the Nature of the Gods* 1.43–56

43. . . . For he [Epicurus] is the only one who saw, first, that the gods exist, because nature herself has impressed a conception of them on the souls of everyone. For what people or race of men is there which does not have, even without being taught, a basic grasp of the gods, which is what Epicurus calls a *prolepsis*, i.e., a kind of outline of the thing [in question], which is antecedently grasped by the mind, and without which nothing can be either understood or investigated or debated? We have learned the force and utility of this line of inference from that divine book of Epicurus on the canon or standard [of truth]. **44.** You see, then, that the point which is the foundation of this investigation has been laid very well indeed. For since the opinion is established not on the basis of some convention or custom or law, but is and remains a solid and harmonious consensus of all men, it is necessary to understand that there are gods, because we have implanted, or rather innate, conceptions of them. For what all men by nature agree about must necessarily be true. So one must concede that the gods exist. Since this point is accepted by virtually everyone, philosophers and laymen alike, let us admit that the following point too is established, that we have this basic grasp, as I said before, or preconception about the gods—for new names must be assigned to new things, just as Epicurus himself referred to a *prolepsis*, which no one had previously designated by this term—**45.** we have, then, this basic grasp, that we consider the gods to be blessed and immortal. And the same nature which gave us an outline of the gods themselves has also inscribed in our minds the notion that they are eternal and blessed. And if this is so, that was a true maxim expounded by Epicurus, that what is blessed and eternal neither has any troubles of its own nor provides them to others, and so is subject to neither anger nor gratitude, since everything of this nature is weak.[23]

Enough would have been said already, if all we were looking for were pious worship of the gods and freedom from superstition; for the excellent nature of the gods would be worshipped by pious men because of that nature's blessedness and eternity (for whatever is excellent is justifiably the object of reverence), and all fears of the anger or power of the gods would have been expelled (for it is understood that anger and gratitude are banned from a blessed and immortal nature, and when these are removed no fears about the beings above hang over us). But in order to confirm this opinion, the mind enquires into the form of god, the kind of activity which characterizes his life, and the mode of operation of his intellect.

46. Nature tells us part of what we need to know about the form of the gods, and the rest is the instruction of reason. For by nature all of us, men of all races, have no other view of the gods but that they have human form; for what other form ever appears to anyone either waking or sleeping? But so that every point will not be referred to the primary notions, reason herself reveals the same thing. **47.** For it seems appropriate that the most excellent nature, excellent either for its blessedness or for its eternity, should also be the most beautiful. So what configuration of the limbs, what arrangement of features, what shape, what general appearance can be more beautiful than the human? ... **48.** But if the human shape is superior to the form of all living things, and a god is a living thing, then certainly he has that shape which is most beautiful of all. And since it is agreed that the gods are most blessed, but no one can be blessed without virtue, nor can virtue exist without reason, nor can reason exist except in a human form, one must concede that the gods have human appearance. **49.** But that appearance is not [really] a body, but a quasi-body, nor does a god have blood, but quasi-blood.

Although Epicurus was so acute in the discovery of these truths and expounded them so subtly that not just anyone could grasp them, still I can rely on your intelligence and expound them more briefly than the subject matter actually demands. Epicurus, then, who not only has a mental vision of hidden and deeply abstruse matters but even manipulates them as though they were tangible, teaches us that the force and nature of the gods is as follows. First, they are perceived not by the

23. Principal Doctrine I.

senses but by the intellect, and not in virtue of some solidity or numerical identity (like those things which because of their resistance he calls *steremnia*), but rather because the images [of the gods] are perceived by virtue of similarity and transference; and since an unlimited series of very similar images arises from innumerable atoms and flows to[24] the gods, our intellect attends to those images and our intelligence is fixed on them with the greatest possible pleasure, and so it grasps the blessed and eternal nature [of the gods]. **50.** It is most worthwhile to reflect long and hard on the tremendous power of infinity, which we must understand is such as to make it possible that all [classes of] things have an exact and equal correspondence with all other [classes of] things. Epicurus calls this *isonomia*, i.e., equal distribution. In virtue of this it comes about that if there is such and such a number of mortal beings, there is no less a number of immortal beings, and if there is an innumerable set of forces which destroy, there ought also to be an infinite set of forces which preserve.

Balbus, you [Stoics] often ask us what the life of the gods is like and how they pass their time. **51.** Well, they spend their time in such a manner that nothing can be conceived which is more blessed or better supplied with all kinds of good things. For a god is idle, is entangled with no serious preoccupations, undertakes no toilsome labour, but simply rejoices in his own wisdom and virtue, being certain that he will always be in the midst of pleasures which are both supreme and eternal. **52.** This god we could properly call blessed, but your [i.e., the Stoic] god is assigned to very hard labour. For if god is the world itself, what can be less restful than to be revolving around the heaven's axis at amazing speed, with not even a moment of rest? But nothing is blessed if it is not at rest. But if there is some god *in* the world to rule and guide it, to maintain the orbits of the heavenly bodies, the changes of the seasons and the ordered variations of [natural] events, to oversee land and sea to ensure that men have lives full of advantages, then surely that god is entangled with burdensome and laborious obligations. **53.** But we claim that happiness is a matter of freedom from disturbance in the mind and leisure from all duties. For the same person who taught us the rest [of this theory] also taught us that the world was produced by nature and that there was no need for someone to make it, and that the task which you say cannot be carried out without divine wisdom is so easy that nature has produced, is producing and will produce an unlimited number of worlds. Since you do not see how nature can do so without [the use of] intelligence, you take refuge like tragedians in [the agency of] god when you cannot work

24. This is the reading of the manuscripts. Many editors accept the simple and attractive emendation "from the gods."

out the conclusion of the plot. **54.** You would certainly not need the assistance of god if you realized the unlimited magnitude of space which is unbounded in all directions; the intellect casts itself into and contemplates this [infinity] and travels so far and wide that it can see no final boundary at which it might stop. So, in this immense length, breadth, and height there flies about an infinite quantity of innumerable atoms, which (despite the interspersal of void) cling to each other and are linked together by their mutual contacts. From this are produced those forms and shapes which you think cannot be produced without the use of a veritable blacksmith's shop! And so you have burdened us with the yoke of an eternal master whom we are to fear by day and by night; for who would not fear an inquisitive and busy god who foresees everything, thinks about and notices everything, and supposes that everything is his own business? **55.** This is the origin of that fated necessity which you call *heimarmene*, and which leads you to say that whatever happens has flowed from an eternal [set of] truth[s] and a continuous chain of causes. But how much is your philosophy worth, if it thinks, like old women—and uneducated ones at that—that everything occurs by fate. Your *mantike* follows too, which is called 'divination' in Latin, because of which we would be drenched in such superstition (if we were prepared to listen to you [Stoics]) that we would have to worship the soothsayers and augurs, the oracular priests and the prophets, and even the diviners! **56.** We are freed from these terrifying fears by Epicurus; we are liberated from them! We do not fear [gods] whom we know do not create trouble for themselves nor for anyone else, and we worship in piety and holiness their excellent and supreme nature.

TEXT 17: *On the Nature of the Gods* 1.69–76 excerpts

69. You [Epicureans] do this all the time. You say something implausible and want to avoid criticism, so you adduce something which is absolutely impossible to support it! It would be better to give up the point under attack than to defend it in such a brazen manner. For example, when Epicurus saw that, if the atoms moved by their own weight straight down, nothing would be in our power, since the atoms' movements would be certain and necessitated, he found a way to avoid necessity—a point which had escaped Democritus' notice. He says that an atom, although it moves downward in a straight line because of its weight and heaviness, swerves a little bit. **70.** This claim is more shameful than the inability to defend the point he is trying to support. He does the same thing in his debate with the dialecticians. They have an accepted teaching to the effect that, in all disjunctions which have the form "either this

or not this," one of the two disjuncts must be true; but Epicurus was
afraid that if a statement such as "Epicurus will either be alive tomorrow
or he will not" were admitted, then one of the two disjuncts would be
necessary. So he denied that all statements of the form "either this or not
this" were necessary. What could be more stupid than this?

Arcesilaus attacked Zeno because, while he himself said that all sense-
perceptions were false, Zeno said that some were false, but not all. Epicurus was afraid that, if one sense-perception were false, none would be
true; so he said that all sense-perceptions were messengers of the truth.
None of these cases shows great cleverness; in order to ward off a minor
blow, he opened himself up to a more serious one.

71. He does the same thing with the nature of the gods. While trying
to avoid saying that [the gods are] a dense compound of atoms, so that he
will not have to admit that they perish and dissipate, he says that the gods
do not have a body, but only a quasi-body, and that they do not have
blood, but only quasi-blood. It is taken to be remarkable if one sooth-
sayer can see another without laughing, but it is even more remarkable,
that you [Epicureans] can restrain your laughter when you are by yourselves. "This is not a body, but a quasi-body"; I could understand what
this would be like if we were talking about waxen images and earthen-
ware figurines. But I cannot understand what quasi-body and quasi-
blood are supposed to be in the case of a god. And neither can you,
Velleius, but you don't want to admit it. . . .

. . . **73.** Now, what do you understand by that quasi-body and quasi-
blood? **74.** Not only do I concede that you understand them better than I,
but I am even happy about it. But when the idea is expressed in words,
what reason is there that Velleius should be able to understand it and
Cotta should not? So I know what body is and what blood is; but in no
way do I understand what quasi-body is or what quasi-blood is. Yet you
do not hide [your view] from me, as Pythagoras used to hide his views
from outsiders, nor do you deliberately speak in riddles like Heraclitus;
rather, to speak frankly between ourselves, you yourself do not understand. **75.** I am aware that you contend that there is a kind of image of
the gods which has nothing solid or dense about it, no definite shape, no
depth, but is refined, light, and translucent. So we will speak of it as we
do of the Venus on Cos: it is not a body but like a body, and the blush
blended with pallor which suffuses [her skin] is not blood but a sort of
semblance of blood. In the same way Epicurean gods are not real things
but semblances of real things.

But suppose that I believe in things which I cannot even understand.
Now show me the outlines and shapes of those shadowy gods of yours!
76. Here you suffer from no lack of arguments designed to show that the

gods have human form. First [is the argument that] our minds contain an
outline and basic grasp of such a nature that when a man thinks about a
god, a human form appears to him; second, that since the divine nature is
better than everything else, it ought also to have the most beautiful form,
and none is more beautiful than the human form; the third argument you
adduce is that no other shape can house an intellect.

TEXT 18: *On the Nature of the Gods* 1.103–110

103. Let us suppose it true, then, as you wish, that god is an image and
semblance of man: what home, what dwelling, what place does he have?
what, indeed, are his activities? in virtue of what is he, as you claim,
happy? For he who is going to be happy ought to both use and enjoy his
own goods. And even inanimate natures have each their own proper
place; for example, earth occupies the lowest place, water floods the
earth, air is above it, and the highest reaches [of the cosmos] are set aside
for the fires of the heavens. Some animals are terrestrial, some aquatic,
some are 'double', as it were, living in both environments; there are even
some which are thought to be born in fire and which often appear flying
about in blazing furnaces! 104. So I ask, first, where does this god of
yours live? next, what cause motivates him to move spatially—if, that is,
he ever does move? then, since it is characteristic of animals that they
pursue what is adapted to their nature, what does god pursue? to what,
pray tell, does he apply his mind and reason? finally, *how* is he happy, *how*
is he eternal?

Whichever of these issues you touch on, it is a weak spot. A theory
with such a bad foundation cannot come to a successful conclusion. 105.
You claimed that the appearance of god is perceived by thought, not the
senses; that it has no solidity and is not numerically identical over time;
that the visual image of it is such that it is discerned by similarity and
transference; that there is an unfailing supply of similar [images] from
the infinite atoms; and that this is why our mind, when directed at these
things, believes that their nature is blessed and eternal. Now, in the name
of the very gods we are talking about, what sort of a claim is this? For if
they are only valid for thought and have no solidity or depth, then what
difference does it make whether we think about a centaur or a god? The
rest of the philosophers call that sort of mental condition an 'empty motion [of the mind]', but you claim that it is the approach and entry of
images into the mind. 106. So when I seem to see Tiberius Gracchus
making a speech on the Capitol and bringing out the voting-urn for the
verdict on Marcus Octavius, I say that is an empty motion of the mind;
but you say that the images of Gracchus and Octavius, which arrived at

the Capitol and came to my mind, persist[25]—and that the same thing happens in the case of god (by whose image our minds are frequently struck) and that this is why the gods are thought of as blessed and eternal.

107. Suppose that there are images which strike our minds; it is still only a certain appearance put before us and not also a reason for it to be happy and eternal. What are these images of yours, and where do they come from? Of course, this free-wheeling idea came from Democritus. But he has been criticized by many, and you [Epicureans] cannot find a way out. The whole theory wobbles and limps. For what could be less plausible than that my mind is struck by images of Homer, Archilochus, Romulus, Numa, Pythagoras, and Plato, let alone by images faithful to the original people! So how do those people [come to my mind]? And whose images are these? Aristotle holds that the poet Orpheus never existed and the Pythagoreans claim that the surviving Orphic poem was written by a certain Cercon. But Orpheus, i.e., on your theory his image, often comes into my mind. 108. And what about the fact that your mind and mine receive different images of the same man? What about the fact that we get images of things which never existed at all and never could have, like Scylla and Charybdis? What about the fact that we get images of people, places, and cities which we have never seen? What about the fact that an image is instantly available as soon as I feel like it? What about the fact that images come unbidden, even to those who are asleep. Velleius' whole theory is nonsense! But you [Epicureans] impose these images not just on our eyes, but on our minds too—that's how recklessly you blather on! 109. And how careless it is. 'There is a steady succession of flowing visual images so that the many produce the appearance of one.' I would be ashamed to admit that I don't understand this, if you yourselves, who defend this stuff, really understood it. For how do you prove that the images move continuously, or if they do move continuously, how are they eternal? 'The infinity of atoms keeps the supply up,' he says. So does the same 'infinity of atoms' make everything eternal? You take refuge in 'equal distribution' (let us use this term for *isonomia*,

---

25. Many translators and editors emend the text of this very difficult sentence. Cicero's hasty composition makes certainty impossible, but the sense seems to be this: images of Gracchus and Octavius travel to the Capitol hill, where their famous confrontation took place in 133 B.C.—almost sixty years before the dramatic date of the dialogue! These images meet at the Capitol and then travel on to Cotta's mind, where together they present him with a visual impression of the event as occurring at the Capitol. The absurdity of such a theory, which Cotta claims the Epicureans are committed to, is evident.

if you will) and say that, since there exists a mortal nature, there must also exist an immortal nature. By that reasoning, since men are mortal, there should be some immortal men too, and since they are born on land, they should also be born in water. 'And because there are forces of destruction, there must also be forces of preservation.' Of course there are. But they preserve things which exist; but I don't think those gods exist. **110.** Anyway, how do all your images of things arise from the atomic bodies? Even if they existed, which they don't, they might perhaps bump into each other and be shaken up by their collisions; but they could not impart form, shape, colour, and life. Therefore you [Epicureans] utterly fail to show that there is an immortal god.

TEXT 19: *Tusculan Disputations* 3.41–42

41. . . . Are these your words, [Epicurus,] or not? In the book which sums up your entire teaching you say this (and here I merely translate, so that no one will think that I am making this up): "Nor do I know what I could understand that good to be, if I set aside the pleasures we get from sex, from listening to songs, from looking at [beautiful] shapes, from smooth motions, or any other pleasures which affect any of man's senses. Nor, indeed, can it be said that only mental rejoicing is [to be counted] among the goods; for this is my understanding of mental rejoicing: it lies in the expectation that our nature will avoid pain while acquiring all those things I just mentioned." **42.** That is exactly what he said, so that anyone can grasp what kind of pleasure Epicurus recognizes. Then a bit later: "I have often asked," he says, "those who are called wise, what they would have left [to put] in the category of goods if they removed those things— unless they were willing to emit empty sounds. I was able to learn nothing from them. And if they wish to burble about virtues and wisdom, they will be referring to nothing except the means by which those pleasures which I mentioned above are produced."

TEXT 20: *Tusculan Disputations* 3.47

The same man says that pleasure does not increase once pain is removed, but that the greatest pleasure lies in not being in pain. . . .

TEXT 21: *On Goals* 1.29–33

29. . . . First, then, he said, I will handle the subject in the manner approved of by the founder of this school: I will settle what it is that we are talking about and what qualities it has, not because I think that you do not know, but so that my discourse might proceed in an orderly and systematic fashion. So, we are asking what is the final and ultimate good, which according to the view of all philosophers ought to be what everything should be referred to, but which should itself be referred to nothing else. Epicurus places this in pleasure, which he claims is the highest good and that pain is the greatest bad thing. And the beginning of his teaching about this is as follows.

30. As soon as each animal is born, it seeks pleasure and rejoices in it as the highest good, and rejects pain as the greatest bad thing, driving it away from itself as effectively as it can; and it does this while it is still not corrupted, while the judgement of nature herself is unperverted and sound. Therefore, he says that there is no need of reason or debate about why pleasure is to be pursued and pain to be avoided. He thinks that these things are perceived, as we perceive that fire is hot, that snow is white, that honey is sweet. None of these things requires confirmation by sophisticated argumentation; it is enough just to have them pointed out. For there is a difference between the rational conclusion of an argument and simply pointing something out; for the former reveals certain hidden and, as it were, arcane facts, while the latter indicates things which are evident and out in the open. Moreover, since there is nothing left if you deprive man of his sense-perception, it is necessary that nature herself judge what is natural and what is unnatural. And what does nature perceive or judge, with reference to what does she decide to pursue or avoid something, except pleasure and pain?

31. There are, however, some members of our school [Epicureans] who want to teach a more subtle form of this doctrine, and they say that it is not sufficient to let sense-perception judge what is good and what is bad, but that the intellect and reason can also understand that pleasure by itself is worth pursuing for its own sake and that pain by itself is to be avoided for its own sake. And so they say that we have this conception, which is, as it were, naturally implanted in our souls, and that as a result of this we perceive that the one is to be pursued and the other to be rejected. But there are other Epicureans too, men with whom I agree, who do not think it right for us to be too sure of our case, since so many philosophers say so much about why pleasure ought not to be counted as a good thing and pain ought not to be counted as a bad thing; they think that one must argue and debate with great care, and employ well researched lines of argument in the dispute about pleasure and pain.

32. But so that you will see the origin of the mistake made by those who attack pleasure and praise pain, I shall open up the whole theory and explain exactly what was said by that discoverer of the truth [Epicurus], who was a kind of architect of the happy life. No one rejects or dislikes or avoids pleasure itself just because it is pleasure, but rather because those who do not know how to pursue pleasure rationally meet with great pains

as a result. Nor again is there anyone who loves, pursues, and wants to acquire pain just because it is pain, but rather because sometimes circumstances of such a nature occur that he can pursue some great pleasure by means of effort and pain. To cite a minor instance: who among us undertakes any demanding regimen of physical training except in order to get some sort of benefit from it? Who, moreover, could justifiably criticize either a man who wished to have the sort of pleasure which is followed by no pains or a man who avoids a pain which serves to produce no pleasure?

33. But we do attack and indeed find most worthy of justified hatred those who are seduced and corrupted by the allures of present pleasures and, being blinded by desire, do not foresee the pains and troubles which they are bound to incur; similarly to blame are those who abandon their duties because of moral weakness, i.e., a tendency to avoid efforts and pains. The distinction here is simple and clear enough. For at a moment of free time, when we have an unrestricted opportunity to select and there is no hindrance to our doing what will be most pleasing to us, [in such circumstances] every pleasure is to be accepted and every pain rejected. But at certain other times, because of the press of responsibilities or the obligations imposed by circumstances it will often happen that pleasures are to be turned down and pains are not to be rejected. And so the wise man sticks with this [principle of] of choosing, that he either acquires greater pleasures by rejecting some of them, or that he avoids worse pains by enduring some of them.

TEXT 22: *On Goals* 1.37–38

37. ... Now I will explain what pleasure is and what it is like, to remove any misunderstandings which inexperienced people may have and to help them to understand how serious, self-controlled, and stern our doctrine is, though it is commonly held to be hedonistic, slack and soft. For we do not just pursue the kind [of pleasure] which stimulates our nature itself with a kind of smoothness and is perceived by the senses with a sort of sweetness, but rather we hold that the greatest pleasure is that which is perceived when all pain is removed. For since when we are freed from pain we rejoice in this very liberation from and absence of annoyance, and since everything in which we rejoice is a pleasure (just as everything which irritates us is a pain), then it is right to call the absence of all pain pleasure. Just as when hunger and thirst are driven out by food and drink, the very removal of annoyance brings with it a resulting pleasure, so in every case too the removal of pain brings with it a consequent pleasure. **38.** So Epicurus did not think that there was some intermediate state between pleasure and pain; for that state which some people think is an intermediate state, viz. the absence of all pain, is not only pleasure but it is even the greatest pleasure. For whoever perceives the state which he is in must in fact be in pleasure or in pain. But Epicurus thinks that the limit for the greatest pleasure is set by the absence of all pain; and though later [i.e., after all pain has been eliminated] pleasure can be varied and adorned, it cannot be increased or augmented.

TEXT 23: *On Goals* 1.55–57

55. I shall give a brief account of what follows from this firm and well established view. There is no possibility of mistake about the limits of good and bad themselves, that is about pleasure and pain; but people do make mistakes in these matters when they are ignorant of the means by which they are produced. Moreover, we say that the pleasures and pains of the mind take their origin from the pleasures and pains of the body (and so I concede the point which you were making recently, that any Epicurean who disagrees is abandoning his case—and I know that there are many who do so, but they are inexperienced); moreover, although mental pleasure and pain do produce good and bad feelings, nevertheless both of them have their origins in the body and take the body as their point of reference; nevertheless, the pleasures and pains of the mind are much greater than those of the body. For with the body we can perceive nothing except what immediately affects it in the present, but with the mind we can also perceive past and future. Even granted that when we feel pain in the body our pain is equal [to what we feel in the mind], still there can be a very large increase [in this pain] if we think that there is some eternal and unlimited bad thing hanging over us. And you may transfer the point to pleasure, so that it is greater if we are not afraid of some such thing. **56.** But this point, at any rate, is already clear, that the greatest pleasure or annoyance in the mind makes much more difference to the production of a blessed or wretched life than either one of them would if they lasted an equally long time in the body. But we do not think that pain immediately follows as soon as pleasure is removed, unless by chance a pain should move into the place of the pleasure; on the other hand we are delighted when pains are eliminated even if no pleasure of the kind which stimulates the senses moves into their place; and from this one can understand just how great a pleasure it is to be free of pain.

57. But just as we are thrilled by the expectation of good things, so too we are pleased by the recollection of good things. But fools are tortured by the recollection of bad things, while wise men enjoy past goods kept fresh by a grateful recollection. For it is a deeply rooted part of human nature to bury in virtually eternal oblivion things which go badly and to recall with satisfaction and contentment things which go well. But when we contemplate past events with a keen and attentive mind, then we feel distress if what we recall was bad, and joy if it was good.

TEXT 24: *On Goals* 2.98

You have often said that no one rejoices or feels pain except because of the body . . . you deny that there is any joy in the mind which is not referred to the body.

TEXT 25: *Tusculan Disputations* 5.93–96

93. You realize, I believe, how Epicurus divided the kinds of desires, perhaps not in a very sophisticated fashion, but usefully at any rate. Some are natural and necessary, some natural and not necessary, some neither [natural nor necessary]. The necessary can be satisfied with next to nothing; for nature's riches are easily acquired. He holds that the second type of desires is not difficult, either to acquire or to do without. The third type he thought should be utterly rejected, since they are clearly vain and not only unnecessary but also unnatural. **94.** At this point the Epicureans make a number of arguments and make excuses one by one for the pleasures of the types which they do not condemn, but which they ⟨do not⟩ seek an abundance of. For they say that even obscene pleasures, which they spend quite a bit of time talking about, are easy, common, and readily available; and that if nature does require them they must be evaluated not with reference to family background, social station, or rank, but only with respect to beauty, age, and figure; and it is not at all difficult to refrain from them, if that is required by poor health, duty, or concern for one's reputation; and in general, that this type of pleasure is to be chosen, if it does not do any harm, but that it never actually benefits anyone. **95.** The upshot of his entire discussion of pleasure is this. He holds that pleasure itself should always be wished for and pursued for its own sake because it is pleasure, and that by the same reasoning pain should always be avoided, just because it *is* pain; and so the wise man will employ a principle of compensation, and will avoid pleasure if it will produce a greater pain and will endure pain if it produces a greater pleasure; and that all pleasing feelings are to be referred to the mind, although they are actually judged by bodily senses. **96.** As a result the body is pleased for only so long as it perceives a present pleasure, while the mind perceives a present pleasure just as much as the body does, but also foresees a pleasure which is coming in the future and does not let a past pleasure slip from its grasp. So the wise man will always have a continuous and interconnected [set of] pleasures, since the expectation of hoped-for pleasures is linked to the memory of pleasures already perceived.

TEXT 26: *On Goals* 1.65–70

65. There remains a topic which is especially important for our present debate, that is friendship. You [the critics] claim that if pleasure is the greatest good there will be no friendship at all. Epicurus indeed says this on the topic:[26] that of all the things which wisdom has contrived which contribute to a blessed life none is more important, more fruitful, or more pleasing than friendship. And he proved this not just in his discourse, but much more clearly by his life and deeds and character. The fictitious tales told by the ancients make it clear how important it is; but in all those stories, so many and so varied and drawn from the most remote periods of antiquity, you could hardly find three pairs of [true] friends, starting with Theseus and finishing up with Orestes. But in just one household—and a small one at that—Epicurus assembled such large congregations of friends which were bound together by a shared feeling of the deepest love. And even now the Epicureans do the same thing.

But let us get back to the point; we do not need to speak of individuals. **66.** I see that the question of friendship has been dealt with in three ways by our school. Some say that our friends' pleasures are not in themselves as worthy of pursuit as are our own (a doctrine which some think undermines the stability of a friendship), but nevertheless they do defend this claim and easily, as I think, get themselves out of their difficulties. Just as we said about the virtues somewhat earlier, so for friendship: they deny that it can be separated from pleasure. For since a solitary life without friends is full of dangerous traps and fear, reason herself advises us to get some friends; and when we do so our mind is reassured and becomes indissolubly linked to the expectation that pleasures will thereby be acquired. **67.** And just as hatred, envy, and contempt are inimical to pleasures, so friendships are not only the most trustworthy supports for our pleasures, but they also produce them, as much for our friends as for ourselves. We enjoy friends not only while they are present with us, but we are also elated by our expectations for the immediate and for the more distant future. Because we cannot possibly secure a stable and long-lasting pleasantness in our life without friendship, and cannot maintain friendship itself unless we cherish our friends just as much as we do ourselves, it follows both that this kind of thing does occur in

26. Principal Doctrine XXVII.

friendship and that friendship is linked with pleasure. For we rejoice at our friends' joys just as much as at our own, and grieve just as much for their anguish. **68**. That is why a wise man will have the same feelings for his friend as for himself and will undertake the same labours for the sake of a friend's pleasure as he would undertake for the sake of his own.

What we said about the way the virtues are always found to be essentially connected to pleasures must also be said about friendship. For Epicurus made a splendid declaration, in almost exactly these words:[27] One and the same doctrine has reassured our minds that there is no eternal or even long-lasting bad thing to fear and has also seen that in this present span of life the most reliable source of protection lies in friendship.

69. There are, however, some Epicureans who are more timid in the face of your abusive criticisms, but are nevertheless pretty sharp-witted; they are afraid that if we believe that friendship is to be pursued for the sake of our own pleasure, all of friendship might seem to be crippled. So they say that people first meet, pair up, and desire to form associations for the sake of pleasure, but that when increasing experience [of each other] has produced the sense of a personal bond, then love flowers to such a degree that even if there is no utility to be gained from the friendship the friends themselves are still loved for their own sake. Indeed, if we typically come to love certain locations, temples, cities, gymnasia, playing fields, dogs, horses, public games (whether with gladiators or animals) just because of familiarity, how much easier and more fitting is it for this to happen in the case of human familiarity?

70. There are also those who say that there is a kind of agreement between wise men, to the effect that they will not cherish their friends less than themselves. We know that this can happen, and that it often does happen; and it is obvious that nothing can be discovered which would be more effective for the production of a pleasant life than this sort of association.

From all of these considerations one can draw the conclusion that not only is the case of friendship not undermined if the highest good is located in pleasure, but also that without this no firm basis for friendship could possibly be discovered.

27. Principal Doctrine XXVIII.

The testimony of Lucretius

The Epicurean Lucretius (first century B.C.) wrote an epic poem *On the Nature of Things* in six books. It should be read in its entirety as crucial evidence for Epicureanism. But two extracts are of particular importance and so are included here.

TEXT 27: *On the Nature of Things* 4.469–499

Moreover, if someone thinks that he knows nothing, he also does not know whether this can be known, since he admits that he knows nothing. So I shall not bother to argue with him, since he is standing on his head already. But nevertheless, conceding that he does know this, I would also ask the following question: since he has never before seen anything true in the world, how does he know what it is to know and what it is not to know? What could have created the conceptions of truth and falsity, and what could have proven that the doubtful is distinct from what is certain? You will discover that the conception of truth was originally created by the senses, and that the senses cannot be refuted. For one must find something with greater authority which could all on its own refute what is false by means of what is true. But what should be given greater authority than the senses? Will reason, which derives from a false sense-perception, be able to contradict them, when it is completely derived from the senses? And if they are not true, all of reason becomes false as well. Will the ears be able to criticize the eyes, or the eyes the touch? Furthermore, will the taste organs of the mouth quarrel with the touch, or will the nose confute it, or the eyes disprove it? In my view, this is not so. For each sense has been allotted its own separate jurisdiction, its own distinct power. And so it is necessary that we separately perceive what is soft and cold or hot and separately perceive the various colours and see the features which accompany colour. Similarly the mouth's taste is separate, and odours come to be separately, and sounds too are separate. And so it is necessary that one set of senses not be able to refute another. Nor, moreover, will they be able to criticize themselves, since they will at all times have to command equal confidence.

TEXT 28: *On the Nature of Things* 2.216–293 excerpts

216. On this topic I want you to learn this too, that when the atoms move straight down through the void by their own weight, they deflect a bit in space at a quite uncertain time and in uncertain places, just enough that you could say that their motion had changed. But if they were not in the habit of swerving, they would all fall straight down through the depths of the void, like drops of rain, and no collision would occur, nor would any blow be produced among the atoms. In that case, nature would never have produced anything.

225. And if by chance someone thinks that heavier atoms, in virtue of their more rapid motion straight through the void, could fall from above on the lighter atoms, and that in this way the blows which generate the productive motions could be produced, he has strayed very far from the true account. For everything which falls through water or light air must fall at a speed proportional to their weights, simply because the bulk of the water and the fine nature of the air can hardly delay each thing equally, but yield more quickly to the heavier bodies, being overwhelmed by them. But by contrast, at no time and in no place can the empty void resist any thing, but it must, as its nature demands, go on yielding to it. Therefore, everything must move at equal speed through the inactive void, though they are not driven by equal weights. Therefore, heavier atoms can never fall upon lighter atoms from above, nor can they by themselves generate blows which will produce change in the motions through which nature produces things. Again and again, that is why it is necessary that the atoms swerve slightly—but not more than the minimum; otherwise, we would seem to be inventing oblique motions and then the plain facts would refute us. For we see this obviously and apparently, that heavy bodies, insofar as they are heavy bodies, cannot move obliquely, when they fall from above, at least not enough that you could observe it. But who could claim to perceive that none of them swerves at all from a perfectly straight path?

251. Finally, if every motion is always linked to another, and new motions always arise from the old in definite order, and the atoms do not produce by swerving a starting point for motion which can break the bonds of fate and prevent one cause from following another from infinity, where does this free will which living things throughout the world have, where, I say, does this will torn from the grasp of the fates come from? Through this we all go where each one's pleasure[28] leads and swerve from our paths at undetermined times and places, just as our minds incline to do. For it is far from doubtful that everyone's own will provides

---

28. 'Will' just above and 'pleasure' here appear in the opposite order in the manuscripts. We follow most editors in reversing them, although some editors defend the transmitted text. In Latin, the two words differ by one letter.

the starting point for these things and that this is the source of motion in our limbs. . . .

284. That is why it is necessary to admit the same thing for the atoms, namely, that there is another cause of motion besides blows [from collisions] and weight, which is the source of our inborn capability [to act freely], since we see that nothing can come from nothing. For the weight of the atoms prevents it from being the case that everything happens as a result of the blows [of collisions], which are like an external force. But that the mind itself does not have an internal necessity in all its actions, and that it is not forced, as though in chains, to suffer and endure, that is what this tiny swerve of the atoms, occurring at no fixed time or place, accomplishes.

The polemic of Plutarch

The later Platonist Plutarch (first to second century A.D.) wrote a polemical treatise *Against Colotes* which contains a wide range of useful information about Epicureanism, as one might expect in a sustained criticism of one of Epicurus' early followers. What follow are excerpts dealing in particular with epistemology and physics.

TEXT 29: Plutarch *Against Colotes* 1109a–1121e, excerpts

(1109a) ... Anyway, he [Colotes] who even held that nothing is any more like this than like that, is using Epicurus' doctrine that all presentations received through the senses are true. (1109b) For if when two people speak and one person says that the wine is dry and the other says that it is sweet, and neither is wrong about his sense-perception, how can the wine be dry rather than sweet? And again, you can see that some people treat a bath as though it were hot and that others treat the same bath as though it were cold. For some ask for cold water to be poured in and others ask for hot. They say that a lady from Sparta came to see Berenike, the wife of Deiotaurus, and when they got close to each other they both turned away, the one nauseated by the [smell of] perfume, the other by the [smell of] butter. So if the one sense-perception is no more true than the other, it is likely both that the water is no more cold than hot and (1109c) that the perfume and the butter are no more sweet-smelling than foul-smelling. For if someone says that the same object of presentation is different for different people, he has missed the fact that he is saying that [the object] is both [at once].

And the much discussed symmetries and harmonies of the pores in the sense organs and the compound mixtures of seeds which they say produce different sense-perceptions of quality in different people by being distributed in all flavours and odours and colours, do these not immediately force things into being 'no more [this than that]' for them? For they reassure those who think that sense-perception deceives on the grounds that they see the same things having opposite effects on perceivers, and instruct them [as follows]: (1109d) since everything is combined and blended together and since different things are designed by nature to fit into different [pores], it is not possible for everyone to touch and grasp the same quality; nor does the object [of sense-perception] affect everyone the same way with all of its parts, but all of them only experience those parts [of an object] with which their sense-organs are symmetrical; so they are wrong to quarrel about whether the object is good or bad or white or not white, supposing that they are supporting their own sense-perceptions by undermining those of other people; but one must not quarrel with even one sense-perception, since all sense-perceptions make contact with something, **(1109e)** each drawing what is compatible and suitable to itself from the compound mixture as though from a spring; and must not assert [things] about the whole when one is in contact with [mere] parts, nor think that everyone has the same experience, but that different people have different experiences according to the differing qualities and powers of it.

So is it time to consider which men do more to inflict 'no more [this than that]' on things than those who proclaim that every sensible object is a blend of all sorts of qualities—'mixed like new wine in the filter'[29]—and who agree that their canons [of truth] would perish and their criterion would completely vanish if they left any object of perception whatsoever pure [and simple] and they did not leave each and every one of them a plurality?

Notice, then, what Epicurus has had Polyaenus (in the *Symposium*) say to him about the heating power of wine. **(1109f)** For when he said, "Epicurus, do you deny that there are heating properties in wine?" he answered, "What need is there to show that wine has heating properties?" And a bit further on: "For wine seems in general not to have heating properties, but a given quantity could be said to have a heating effect on this individual person."

And again, suggesting the cause [for this], he attributed it to **(1110a)** compactions and dispersions of atoms and to commixtures of and linkages with other atoms in the mixture of wine with the body; and then he adds: "that is why one must not say that wine has heating properties in general, but that a given quantity has a heating effect on a nature of this type which is in this sort of condition, or that a given amount could have a cooling effect on this [other] nature. For in such an aggregate [as wine] there are also the sort of natures from which coolness might be produced, or which being linked appropriately with other natures, would produce the nature of coolness. Hence, people are deceived, some into saying that wine in general has cooling properties, others that it has heating properties."

But he who says that the majority are deceived when they suppose that what heats things has heating properties, or that what cools things has

29. A fragment from an unknown Greek tragedy, 420 Nauck.

cooling properties, is himself deceived, **(1110b)** unless he believes that it follows from what he says that each thing is no more like this than like that. And he adds that wine often does not enter the body with heating or cooling properties, but that when the mass has been set in motion and the rearrangement of bodies has occurred, sometimes the atoms which produce heat assemble in one place and by their numbers produce heat and fever in the body, and sometimes they are expelled and [so] chill it.

It is obvious that these arguments can be used against everything which is generally said or believed to be bitter, sweet, purgative, soporific, or bright, on the grounds that nothing **(1110c)** has its own independent quality or power when it is in bodies, nor is it active rather than passive, but rather takes on different features and mixtures in various bodies.

For Epicurus himself, in book two of his *Against Theophrastus*, says that colours are not natural properties of bodies, but are produced by certain orderings and positions [of the atoms] relative to our vision; yet he says that, by this argument, body is no more colourless than it is coloured. And earlier he had written this, word for word: "but even without this part [of my theory] I do not know how one can say that those things which are in the dark have colour. And yet, when there is a dark cloud of air [i.e., fog] evenly wrapped around things, **(1110d)** it is often the case that some men perceive differences in colours while others do not because of the dullness of their vision; again, when we go into a dark house we do not see colours, but after we have stayed for a while we do." Therefore, no body will be said to have colour rather than not to have it.

And if colour is relative, so too will white and blue be relative, and if these, so too sweet and bitter; consequently it will be true to predicate of every quality that it no more exists than does not exist: for the object will be like this for people in one condition, but not for those who are not. **(1110e)** So Colotes ends up pouring over himself and his master the very mud and confusion in which he says those people wallow who assert that things are 'no more this than that'.

So is this the only place where this fine fellow shows that he "teems with sores though he tries to heal others"?[30] Not at all. In his second accusation [Colotes] fails even more miserably to notice how he drives Epicurus, along with Democritus, outside the pale of normal life. For he claims that Democritus' dicta, "colour is by convention and sweet is by convention" and compounds are by convention and so forth, but "in truth there are void and atoms," are opposed to sense perception; and

---

30. Euripides fr. 1086 Nauck.

that anyone who clings to and uses this theory could not even think of himself as human or as alive.

I have no criticism to make of this argument, and I claim that these [Democritean] views are as inseparable from Epicurus' opinions as they themselves say the shape and weight are from the atom. For what does Democritus say? that substances infinite in number, indivisible and indestructible and, moreover, qualitiless and impassible, are scattered about and move in the void; (1111a) and when they approach one another or collide or get tangled up with each other they appear, because they are aggregated, as water, fire, a plant, or a man; and that everything is what he calls atomic 'forms' and is nothing else. For there is no coming-into-being from what-is-not, and from what-is nothing could come to be since atoms can neither suffer nor change due to their solidity. Hence colour does not exist, [for it would have to be] made up of colourless things, nor do nature and soul exist, [for they would have to be] made up of qualitiless and impassive things.

So Democritus is to be criticized not for conceding what follows from his principles, but for assuming principles from which these conclusions follow. (1111b) For he ought not to have posited that the primary entities were unchangeable, but having made this postulate he ought to have seen that he has eliminated the genesis of all qualities. The most brazen position of all is to see the absurdity and to deny it. So Epicurus makes the most brazen claim, saying that he posits the same principles but does not say that "colour is by convention" and [so too] sweet and bitter and the qualities. If "does not say" means "does not admit," then he is up to his old tricks. For while destroying divine providence he says that he leaves piety intact, and while choosing friendship for the sake of pleasure he says that he would suffer the greatest pains for the sake of his friends, and he says that he postulates that the totality is unlimited but that he does not eliminate up and down. This sort of behaviour is not right even when one is joking over a drink: (1111c) to take a cup and drink as much as one wants and then to give back what is left. In argument one must recall this wise maxim: the beginnings may not be necessitated, but the consequences are. So it was not necessary to postulate—or rather to steal [the doctrine] from Democritus—that the principles of the universe are atoms; but when once he postulated the doctrine and prided himself on its superficial plausibility, then he ought to have drained its difficulties to the last drop too, or showed us how bodies which have no qualities produced most varied qualities just by coming together in a compound. For example, where did you get what is called hot and how did it come to be an attribute of your atoms, (1111d) which neither came [into the compound] already having heat, nor did they become hot by their conjunction? For the former is characteristic of something which has a quality, and the latter of something which is naturally prone to be affected; but you say that neither of these is appropriate for your atoms because they are indestructible.

. . . (1112e) . . . When Epicurus says, "the nature of existing things is bodies and place," should we interpret him as meaning that nature is something distinct from and in addition to the existing things, (1112f) or as referring just to the existent things and to nothing else? just as, for instance, he is in the habit of calling the void itself 'the nature of void' and, by Zeus, the totality [of things] the 'nature of the totality'.

. . . (1114a) Yet by saying that the totality is one he somehow prevented us from living. For when Epicurus says that the totality is unlimited and ungenerated and indestructible and neither grows nor shrinks, he discourses about the totality as though it were some one thing. In the beginning of his treatise [*On Nature*] he suggests that the nature of existing things is bodies and void, and though it is one nature, he yet divided it into two. One of these is really nothing, but you call it intangible and void and incorporeal.

. . . (1118d) . . . For if, as they think, a man is the product of both, a body of this sort and a soul, then he who investigates the nature of soul is investigating the nature of man by way of its more important principle. And let us not learn from Socrates, that sophistical boaster, that the soul is hard to understand by reason and ungraspable by sense-perception, but rather let us learn it from these wise men who get only as far as the corporeal powers of the soul, by virtue of which it provides the body with warmth and softness and tension, (1118e) when they cobble together its substance out of something hot and something breathlike and something airy, and they do not get to the most important part, but give up. For that in virtue of which it judges and remembers and loves and hates and in general the intelligent and reasoning part, this they say comes to be from a kind of 'nameless' quality.

. . (1119f) . . . Who makes worse mistakes in dialectic than you [Epicureans], who completely abolish the class of things said [*lekta*], which give substance to discourse and leave only [mere] utterances and the external things, saying that the intermediate class of 'signified things' (by means of which learning, (1120a) teaching, basic grasps, conceptions, impulses, and assents all occur) does not exist at all?

. . . (1121a) For he [i.e., Colotes] is satisfied with and welcomes arguments when they are used in Epicurus' writings, but does not understand or recognize them when they are used by others. For those who say that when a round image strikes us, or another which is bent, the sense receives a true imprint, and who do not allow the further claim that the tower is round and that the oar is bent—these men affirm their own experiences and impressions but are unwilling to agree that external objects are like this. But just as that group must refer to 'being affected horsewise or wallwise' but not to a horse or a wall, **(1121b)** in the same way they must say that the visual organ is 'affected roundly or anglewise' but not that the oar is bent or that the tower is round. For the image by which the visual organ is affected is bent, but the oar from which the image came is not bent. So since the [internal] experience is different from the external object, either our conviction must limit itself to the experience or, if it makes the further claim that 'it is' in addition to 'it appears', it must be refuted. And their vociferous and indignant claim about sense-perception, that it does not say that the external object is warm but that the experience in [the perception] is like that—**(1121c)** is this not the same as what is said about taste, viz. that he denies that the external object is sweet but says that an experience and motion in the [organ of] taste is of this character? And he who says that he receives a presentation in the shape of a man, but that he does not perceive whether there is a man, now where did he get the inspiration [for such an idea]? Was it not from those who say that they receive a curved presentation, but that the visual organ does not make the additional pronouncement that it is curved, nor even that it is round, but that a certain round impression and imprint has occurred in it?

'Yes, by Zeus,' someone will say, 'but when I approach the tower and when I take hold of the oar, I will pronounce the one to be straight and the other to be polygonal, but the other [philosopher] will agree to seeming and appearance, but nothing more, even if he does get close [to the object].' Yes, by Zeus, **(1121d)** because, dear sir, he [Epicurus] sees what follows [from his position] better than you do, and he sticks with it: viz. that every presentation on its own account is equally trustworthy and that no presentation is preferable to another, but that all are of equal value. But you are giving up the principle that all [perceptions] are true and that none is unreliable or false if you think that based on these one ought to further pronounce regarding external objects, but did not trust them for anything beyond the experience itself. For if they are equally trustworthy when they appear close up and when they are distant, either it is right to allow judgement to pronounce further, based on all of them or not to allow this for even these. But if there is a difference in the experience according as we are standing at a distance or close by, then it is false to say that one presentation or sense-perception **(1121e)** is not clearer than another; similarly, the testimony for and testimony against about which they speak have nothing to do with sense-perception, but rather with opinion. So, if they urge us to follow these and to pronounce on external objects, they make opinion judge what is the case and make sense-perception experience the appearances, and they transfer the deciding power from what is in all circumstances true to what is often mistaken.

Short fragments and testimonia from known works

From *On Nature*

See TEXT 29, 1114a and 1112ef above.

TEXT 30: Sextus *M* 9.333 (75 U)

Epicurus was in the habit of calling the nature of bodies and of the void [the] universe and [the] totality indifferently. For at one point he says, "The nature of the universe is bodies and void."

TEXT 31: Vatican Scholiast on Dionysius Thrax, *Grammatici Graeci* 1.3, p. 116.7–12 (Hilgard) (92 U)

And although Epicurus always made use of general outlines [of the senses of words], he showed that definitions are more worthy of respect by using definitions instead of general outlines in the treatise on physics; for he used definitions when he divided the totality into the atomic and the void, saying that "the atomic is a solid body which has no share of void included in it; ⟨and⟩ void is an intangible nature", i.e., not subject to touch.

TEXT 32: From books 12 and 13 of *On Nature* (Arrighetti 27 and 28, 84, 87, 88 U = Philodemus *On Piety*)

And in book 12 of the *On Nature* he says that the first men got conceptions of indestructible natures. . . .
As in book 12 he also criticizes Prodicus and Diagoras and Critias and others, saying that they are madmen and lunatics, and he compares them to bacchic revellers. . . .
In book 13 [he mentions] the congeniality which god feels for some and the alienation [for others].

TEXT 33: From book 32. An unknown author. Arrighetti 32.

In book 32 he offers a brief and summary definition of what was explained at great length elsewhere: "For," he says, "the soul could be said to be a certain nature."

TEXT 34: From book 25.[31]

From the very beginning we have seeds which lead us, some to these things, some to those things, and some to both; they are always [the seeds of] actions, and thoughts and dispositions, and are greater or fewer in number. Consequently, what we develop—such or such [actions, thoughts, and dispositions]—is, right from the first, quite simply a result of us; and the influences which by necessity flow from the environment through our passages are at some point up to us and to the opinions which come from within us ... [here there is a long lacuna].

... the natural imprint similarly to the empty pores ... of the same peculiarities ... in every case [lacuna of about 12 words] of which the experiences do not cease to occur ... to admonish and quarrel with each other and try to change each other's character, as though they had in themselves the responsibility for [their characters] and [such responsibility lay] not just in the original [condition of] the compound, and in the necessity which comes mechanically from the environment and the influx [of atoms]. For if one were to attribute to admonishing and being admonished the mechanical necessity of what always on any occasion [happens to] affect oneself, one would never in this way come to an understanding [lacuna of a few words] by blaming or praising.

But if one were to do this, one would be leaving the very action which, being in our power, creates the basic grasp of responsibility, and thereby in some respect having changed his doctrine [long lacuna, of 45 or 50 words] of such error. For this sort of argument is upside-down and can never prove that all things are like what are called 'necessitated events'. But he quarrels about this very topic on the assumption that his opponent is responsible for being foolish. And if he [goes on] indefinitely saying again [and again], always on the basis of arguments, that he does *this* by necessity, he is not reasoning it out [properly] as long as he attributes to himself responsibility for reasoning well and to his opponent responsibility for reasoning badly. But if he were not to stop [attributing responsibility] for what he does to himself and [rather] to assign it to necessity, he would not ... [lacuna of about 30 words]

[But] if he is only changing the word when he refers to what we call "through our own [agency]" by the name of necessity and will not show

---

31. Formerly thought to be from book 35. This discussion on determinism should be compared with the discussions of the swerve above. We translate the text prepared by David Sedley and published in his article 'Epicurus' Refutation of Determinism' in *Syzetesis* (Naples 1983) 11–51.

that it is in virtue of a basic grasp of a sort which produces deficient outlines that we talk about responsibility through our own [agency], he would neither [lacuna of about 25 words] to occur, but to call even necessity empty, from what you people say. And if someone does not say this and has no auxiliary [cause] in us and no inclination to dissuade us from things which we do, while calling the responsibility for them 'through our own agency', but giving everything which we now assert that we do while naming the responsibility for it as being 'through our own agency' the name of 'foolish necessity', then he will merely be altering the name. And he will not change any of our actions, in the way in which in some cases he who sees what sort of things are necessitated usually dissuades those who are eager to act in defiance of force. And the intellect will endeavour to find out which sort of thing one is to think an action is, which we do somehow from within ourselves, but which we are not eager to do.

For he has no choice but to say that what sort [of action] is necessitated [and what not] [lacuna of about 40 words] ... among the most senseless. If someone does not forcibly insist on this or again set out what he is refuting and what he is introducing, only the wording is changed, as I have been going on about for a while now.

But those who first gave a sufficient causal account and were not only superior to their predecessors but also many times over superior to their successors, failed to notice—despite the fact that they removed serious difficulties in many areas—that they gave causal accounts for everything by referring to necessity and mechanistic explanation. And the very argument which explains this doctrine disintegrated, and the fellow did not notice that it brought his actions into conflict with his opinions; and that if a kind of distraction did not possess him while he acted, he would be constantly disturbing himself; and that insofar as his opinion held sway, he got into the worst sort of problems, but insofar as it did not hold sway he was filled with internal strife because of the contradiction between his actions and his opinion. . . .

From the *Puzzles*

TEXT 35: Plutarch *Against Colotes* 1127d (18 U, 12 [1] A)

. . . For in the *Puzzles* Epicurus asks himself whether the wise man will do some things which the laws forbid, if he knows that he will escape detection. And he answers: "the plain statement [of the answer] is not easy", i.e., I will do it but I do not wish to admit it.

From *On the Goal*

TEXT 36: Plutarch *A Pleasant Life* 1089d (68 U, 22 [3] A)

. . . "For the stable condition (*katastema*) of the flesh and the reliable expectation concerning this contains the highest and most secure joy, for those who are able to reason it out."

TEXT 37: Athenaeus *Deipnosophists* 12, 546ef (67 U, 22 [1, 4] A)

Not only Aristippus and his followers, but also Epicurus and his welcomed kinetic pleasure; and I will mention what follows, to avoid speaking of the "storms" [of passion] and the "delicacies" which Epicurus often cites, and the "titillations" and the "stimuli" which he mentions in his *On the Goal*. For he says: "For I at least do not even know what I should conceive the good to be, if I eliminate the pleasures of taste, and eliminate the pleasures of sex, and eliminate the pleasures of listening, and eliminate the pleasant motions caused in our vision by a visible form."

. . . And in his *On the Goal* he again [says]: "One must honour the noble, and the virtues and things like that, *if* they produce pleasure. But if they do not, one must bid them goodbye."

From the *Symposium*:
See TEXT 29, 1109e–1110b above.

From *Against Theophrastus*:
See TEXT 29, 1110cd above.

Fragments of Epicurus' letters

TEXT 38: Plutarch *On Living the Inconspicuous Life* 1128f–1129a
           (106–7 U, 98 A)

(1128f) Moreover, if you advise good men to be inconspicuous and to be unknown . . . give yourself [Epicurus] the same advice first. Don't write to your friends in Asia, don't address the visitors from Egypt, (1129a) don't keep watch over the youths in Lampsacus, don't send books to all, male and female alike, showing off your wisdom, and don't give written instructions for your burial.

TEXT 39: Plutarch *Against Colotes* 1117a (116 U, 42 A)

(1117a) . . . In the letter to Anaxarchus he wrote as follows: "I summon you to constant pleasures, and not to virtues, which provide [only] empty, pointless, and disturbing expectations of rewards."

TEXT 40: Plutarch *A Pleasant Life* 1101ab (120 U)

(1101a) . . . They argue with those who eliminate pains and tears and lamentations for the deaths of friends, and they say that the kind of freedom from pain which amounts to insensitivity[32] is the result of another and greater bad thing, savagery or an unadulterated lust for fame and madness, and that this is the reason why it is better to suffer something and experience pain, and by Zeus even to weep copiously, swoon and [experience] all the sentiment which they indulge in and [even] write about, and so come to seem tender and given to friendship. (1101b) For Epicurus said this in lots of other places and he also [said it] about the death of Hegesianax when he wrote to his father Dositheus and to Pyrson, the brother of the deceased. For recently I chanced to go through his letters.

TEXT 41: *Letter to Idomeneus:* Diogenes Laertius 10.22 (138 U, 52 A)

"I write this to you while experiencing a blessedly happy day, and at the same time the last day of my life. Urinary blockages and dysenteric discomforts afflict me which could not be surpassed for their intensity. But against all these things are ranged the joy in my soul produced by the recollection of the discussions we have had. Please take care of the children of Metrodorus in a manner worthy of the good disposition you have had since adolescence towards me and towards philosophy."

TEXT 42: Seneca *Letters on Ethics* 22.5–6 (133 U, 56 A)

Read . . . the letter of Epicurus which is entitled "To Idomeneus"; he requests Idomeneus that he flee and hurry as much as he can, before some greater force has a chance to intervene and take away his freedom to 'retreat'. 6. The same man also adds that nothing should be undertaken except when it can be undertaken fittingly and on a good occasion. But when that long-awaited moment comes, he says one must make one's exit. He instructs the man considering escape not to be negligent, and expresses the hope that there is a salutary escape, even from the most difficult situations, providing we neither hasten before the right time nor hold back when the time has come.

---

32. The term used is *apathes*, the Stoic word for freedom from destructive passions.

TEXT 43: Plutarch *Against Colotes* 1127de (134 U)

(1127d) Again, I think, in writing to Idomeneus he urges him not to live as a slave to laws and opinions, as long as they do not occasion troubles caused by a blow from one's neighbour. So if those who abolish laws and political institutions abolish human life, **(1127de)** then this is what Epicurus and Metrodorus do; for they urge their adherents to avoid public life and express disgust for those who participate in it, abusing the earliest and wisest lawgivers and urging contempt for the laws, providing there is no fear of beatings and punishment.

TEXT 44: A Deathbed Letter (from Philodemus, *Pragmateiai* 31
           Diano; 177 U, 78 A)

"As I write this, it is the seventh day that I have been unable to urinate and have had pains of the kind which lead to death. So, if anything should happen, take care of Metrodorus' children for four or five years, spending no more on them than you now spend on me in a year."

TEXT 45: Stobaeus *Anthology* 3.17.23 (vol. 3 p. 495 W-H; 135 U,
           53 A)

"If you wish to make Pythocles wealthy, do not give him more money; rather, reduce his desires."

TEXT 46: Plutarch *Against Colotes* 1117e (130 U, 54 A)

"So send us some offerings for the care of our sacred body, on your own behalf and that of the children. For so it occurs to me to say to you."

TEXT 47: Seneca *Letters on Ethics* 21.3 (132 U, 55 A)

"If you are affected by glory, my letters will make you more famous than all those things which you cherish and because of which you are cherished."

TEXT 48: Stobaeus *Anthology* 3.17.13 (vol. 3 p. 492 W-H; 135a U,
           58 A)

"We have been keen for self-sufficiency, not so that we should employ inexpensive and plain fare under all circumstances, but so that we can be of good cheer about them."

TEXT 49: Seneca *Letters on Ethics* 18.9 (158 U, 83 A)

. . . He certainly says this in the letter which he wrote to Polyaenus in the archonship of Charinus; and indeed he boasts that he could be fed for less than an obol, but that Metrodorus, because he had not yet made so much [moral] progress, required an entire obol.

TEXT 50: Athenaeus *Deipnosophists* 13 588ab (117 U, 43 A)

"I congratulate you, sir, because you have come to philosophy free of any taint of culture."

TEXT 51: Diogenes Laertius 10.6 (163 U, 89 A)

And in his letter to Pythocles,[33] he writes, "O blessed one, spread your sails and flee all forms of culture."

TEXT 52: Plutarch *A Pleasant Life* 1097cd (183 U, 99 A)

(1097c) . . . when [Epicurus] wrote to his friends, "you took care of us in a godlike and magnificent fashion as regards the provision of food, and (1097d) you have given proofs which reach to heaven of your good will towards me."

TEXT 53: Seneca *Letters on Ethics* 9.1 (174 U)

You want to know whether Epicurus is right to criticize, as he does in one letter, those who say that a wise man is self-sufficient and so does not need a friend. Epicurus makes this objection against Stilpo and those [i.e., the Stoics] who held that the highest good is a soul free of passions.

TEXT 54: Seneca *Letters on Ethics* 9.8 (175 U)

. . . Although a wise man is self-sufficient, he will still want to have a friend, if for no other reason, in order to exercise his friendship, so that so great a virtue might not go to waste; not for the reason which Epicurus gave in this very letter, so that he might have someone to attend to him when sick, and to help him when he is thrown into prison or is impoverished, but so that he might have someone whom he might himself attend when that person is sick and whom he might free from imprisonment by his enemies.

TEXT 55: Philodemus *On Piety* 126 Gomperz (387 U, 114 A)

Again: "let us sacrifice to the gods," he says, "piously and well, as is appropriate, and let us do everything well according to the laws, but [let us do so] not disturbing them at all with our opinions on the topic of

33. Not the same letter translated above.

those who are best and most majestic; again, we say that it is even right [to do this] on the basis of the opinion which I was discussing. For in this way, by Zeus, it is possible for a mortal nature to live like Zeus, as it appears."

TEXT 56: Philodemus *On Piety* 105 Gomperz (157 U, 86 A)

Moreover, in his letter to Polyaenus he says that one should join in the celebration of the festival of the Anthesteria. For one must remember the gods as being the causes of many good things.

TEXT 57: Philodemus *On Piety* 125 Gomperz (116 A)

". . . for the others, and I asked them to display benevolence to other men at all times."

TEXT 58: Diogenes Laertius 10.11 (182 U, 123 A)

"Send me a small measure of cheese, so that when I want to have a feast I shall be able to do so."

TEXT 59: Stobaeus *Anthology* 3.17.33 (vol. 3 p. 501 W-H; 181 U, 124 A)

"I revel in the pleasure of my poor body, employing water and bread, and I spit upon the pleasures of extravagance, not for their own sake, but because of the difficulties which follow from them."

TEXT 60: Seneca *Letters on Ethics* 20.9 (206 U, 125 A)

"Your discourse will appear more impressive, believe you me, if you are lying on a cheap bed and wearing rags. For it will not only be uttered, then, but proven."

TEXT 61: Porphyry *To Marcella* 29 (207 U, 126 A)

"It is better for you to have confidence [about the future] while lying on a cheap bed than to be disturbed while possessing a golden couch and an extravagant table."

TEXT 62: Seneca *Letters on Ethics* 7.11 (208 U, 129 A)

"I write this for you, not for the many; for we are for each other a sufficiently big audience."

TEXT 63: *Gnomologium Parisinum* 1168 f. 115 r. (187 U, 131 A)

"I never desired to please the many, for I did not learn the things which please them, and what I did learn was far removed from their perception."

TEXT 64: Didymus Caecus *Commentary on Ecclesiastes* 24.8–11
          (133 A)

For he writes [in his letter] to Idomeneus that the wise man uses circumstances in a way different from he who is not wise, and he adds: "Then you were not wise, but now you have been zealous to become so. So reflect on the quality of your former life and of your present life, [to see] if you bore disease then as you do now or if you were in control of wealth as you are now in control of it."

Short fragments and testimonia from uncertain works

Logic and epistemology

TEXT 65: Philodemus *Pragmateiai* 29 Diano (212 U, 137 A)

". . . bringing your letter and the reasoning which you had carried out concerning men who could see neither the analogy which obtains between the phenomena and the unseen [realities] nor the consistency which exists between the senses and the unseen [realities] and again the testimony against . . ."

TEXT 66: Seneca *Letters on Ethics* 89.11 (242 U)

The Epicureans held that there are two parts of philosophy, physics and ethics; they got rid of logic. Then since they were forced by the very facts to distinguish what was ambiguous and to refute falsities lying hidden under the appearance of truth, they themselves also introduced that topic which they call 'on judgement and the criterion' [i.e., canonic]; it is [just] logic by another name, but they think that it is an accessory part of physics.

TEXT 67: Sextus *M* 8.9 (244 U)

But Epicurus said that all sensibles were true and existing—for there was no difference between saying that something is true and that it is an existing object. And that is why, in giving an outline [definition] of the true and the false, he says, "that which is such as it is said to be is true" and "that which is not such as it is said to be is false."

TEXT 68: Sextus *M* 7.203–16 (247 U)

203. Epicurus says that there are two things which are linked to each other, presentation and opinion, and that of these presentation, which he also calls 'clear fact,' is always true. For just as the primary feelings, i.e., pleasure and pain, come to be from certain productive factors and in accordance with the productive factors themselves (for example, pleasure comes to be from pleasant things and pain from painful things, and what causes pleasure can never fail to be pleasant, nor can what produces pain not be painful; but rather, it is necessary that what gives pleasure should be pleasant and that what gives pain should in its nature be painful), so [too] in the case of presentations, which are feelings in us: what causes each of them is presented in every respect and unqualifiedly, and since it is presented it cannot help but exist in truth just as it is presented [as being]. ... [There is a lacuna here.] ... that it is productive of presentation.

204. And one must reason similarly for the individual [senses]. For what is visible not only is presented as visible but also is such as it is presented [as being]; and what is audible is not only presented as audible but also is like that in truth; and similarly for the rest. Therefore, it turns out that all presentations are true. And reasonably so. **205.** For if, the Epicureans say, a presentation is true if it comes from an existing object and in accordance with the existing object, and [if] every presentation arises from the object presented (which is existent) and in accordance with the presented object itself, [then] necessarily every presentation is true.

206. Some people are deceived by the difference between the presentations which seem to come from the same perceptible, for example, a visible thing, according to which [i.e., the difference] the object is presented as being of varying colour or varying shape or as different in some other way. For they supposed that one of the presentations which differ and conflict in this way must be true and the one derived from the opposites must be false. This is foolish and the product of men who do not have a comprehensive view of the nature of [lit. in] things.

207. Let us make our case for visible things. For the solid object is not seen in its entirety, but [we see only] the colour of the solid. And of the colour some is on the solid itself, as in things seen from close by and things seen from a moderate distance, and some lies outside the solid and in the adjacent places, as in things observed from a great distance. And since this [colour] changes in the intermediate [space] and takes on its own shape it produces the sort of presentation which is just like what it [i.e., the colour] itself is really like. **208.** So, just as the sound which is heard is not that in the bronze instrument being struck nor that in the mouth of the man shouting, but rather is that which strikes our sense [organ]; and as no one says that he who hears a faint voice from a distance hears it falsely since when he comes closer he grasps it as being louder; so I would not say that the vision speaks falsely because it sees the tower as small and round from a distance but from close up sees it as larger and square. **209.** But rather [I would say] that [the vision] tells the truth, since when the object of perception appears to it [as] small and of such a shape it is genuinely small and of such a shape (for the edges of the images are broken off by the movement through the air), and when it again appears big and of a different shape, again it is in a similar manner big and has that different shape—the object being, however, now not the

same in the two cases. For it remains for distorted opinion to think that
the same object of presentation was observed from close up and from a
distance.

210. It is a property of sense-perception to grasp only that which is
present and stimulating it, such as colour, but not to decide that the object here and the object over there are different. So for these reasons all
presentations are true ⟨though not all opinions are true⟩ but have some
differences [among them]. For some of these [opinions] are true and
some are false, since they are our judgements upon presentations and we
judge some things correctly and some badly, either by adding and attach-
ing something to the presentations or by subtracting something from
them—in general terms, by falsifying the non-rational sense-perception.

211. Therefore, according to Epicurus, some opinions are true and
some are false; those which are testified for and those which are not
testified against by clear facts are true, while those which are testified
against and those which are not testified for by clear facts are false. **212.**
'Testimony for' is a grasp, by means of clear facts, that the object of
opinion is such as it once was thought to be. For example, when Plato is
approaching from the distance I guess and opine, because of the distance, that it is Plato; but when he approached there was further testimony that it was Plato (since the distance was reduced) and [finally] the
clear facts themselves testified to it. **213.** 'Lack of testimony against' is
the consistency of the non-evident thing which is the object of supposition and opinion with what is apparent. For example, when Epicurus says
that there is void, which is a non-evident object, he confirms this through
a clear fact, i.e., motion; for if void does not exist, then motion ought not
to exist, since the moving body would have no place to shift into because
everything [would] be full and dense; **214.** consequently, since there is
motion what is apparent does not testify against the non-evident thing
which is the object of opinion. 'Testimony against', however, is something in conflict with 'lack of testimony against'. For it is the joint elimi-
nation of what is apparent along with the supposed non-evident thing.
For example, the Stoic says that there is no void, holding that it is something non-evident, and thus along with this supposed fact one ought to
eliminate what is apparent, by which I mean motion; for if there is no
void it follows necessarily that there is no motion, according to the mode
[of argument] which we have already indicated. **215.** Similarly too, 'lack
of testimony for' is in opposition to 'testimony for'. For it [i.e., the lack of
testimony for] is the evidence through clear facts that the object of opinion is not just as it was opined to be. For example, when someone is
approaching from afar we guess, because of the distance, that it is Plato;
but when the distance is reduced we realize through clear facts that it is

not Plato. And this sort of thing turns out to be 'lack of testimony for'. For the object of opinion was not testified for by what was apparent. **216.** Hence, testimony for and lack of testimony against are the criterion of something's being true, while lack of testimony for and testimony against are [the criterion of something's being] false. And clear facts are the foundation and cornerstone of all [four of these].

TEXT 69: Aetius 4.9.5 = *Dox.Gr.* p. 396 (248 U)

Epicurus [says] that every sense-perception and every presentation is true, but that some opinions are true and some are false.

TEXT 70: Sextus *M* 8.63–64 (253 U)

63. Epicurus said that all sensibles are true and that every presentation comes from something existing and is of the same sort as that which stimulates the sense-perception. He also says that those who say that some presentations are true and some are false are led astray because they are not able to distinguish opinion from clear fact. At least in the case of Orestes, when he thought he saw the Furies, his sense-perception which was stimulated by images was true (for the images did exist), whereas his mind, in thinking that the Furies were solid [objects], held a false opinion. **64.** And further, he says, the aforementioned [philosophers] who introduce a difference among presentations are not able to convince [us] that it is the case that some of them are true and some false. For they will not be able to instruct us in such a matter by means of an appearance (for appearances are just what is being investigated), nor by means of something non-evident (for that which is non-evident has to be demonstrated by means of an appearance).

TEXT 71: Clement of Alexandria *Stromates* 2.4,16.3 p. 121 Stählin (255 U)

Indeed, Epicurus, who more than anyone prefers pleasure to truth, supposes that a basic grasp is the [basis] of the intellect's conviction; he defines a basic grasp as an application [of the intellect] to something clear and to the clear conception of the thing, and [holds] that no one can either investigate or puzzle over, nor even hold an opinion or even refute [someone], without a basic grasp.

TEXT 72: Sextus *M* 11.21 (255 U)

According to the wise Epicurus it is not possible to investigate or [even] to be puzzled without a basic grasp.

TEXT 73: Sextus *M* 8.258 (259 U)

... We see that there are some who have abolished the existence of 'things said' [*lekta*], not just [philosophers] from other schools, such as the Epicureans, but even Stoics such as Basilides and his followers, who thought that no incorporeal [entity] exists.

TEXT 74: Sextus *M* 8.13 (259 U)

But the followers of Epicurus and Strato the natural philosopher leave [in existence] only two [such entities], the signifier and the object, and so they appear to belong to the second group and to make the true and the false a matter of the utterance [and not the things said, i.e., *lekta*].

TEXT 75: Sextus *M* 8.177 (262 U)

... For Epicurus and the leaders of his school said that the sign was sensible, while the Stoics said that it was intelligible.

Physics and theology

TEXT 76: Pseudo-Plutarch *Stromates* 8 = *Dox.Gr.* p. 581 (266 U)

... in the totality [of things] nothing unprecedented happens beyond [what has happened in] the unlimited time which has already passed.

TEXT 77: Aetius 1.3.18 = *Dox.Gr.* p. 285–6 (267, 275 U)

Epicurus, the son of Neocles and an Athenian, philosophized in the manner of Democritus and said that the principles of existing things are bodies which can be contemplated by reason, which do not participate in void and are ungenerated and indestructible, since they can neither be broken nor be compounded [or: arranged] out of parts, nor be altered in their qualities. They are contemplated by reason. Anyway, they move in the void and through the void. And the void itself is infinite, and so are the bodies. Bodies have these three properties: shape, size, weight. Democritus said that there were two, size and shape, but Epicurus added weight to these as a third. For, he says, it is necessary that the bodies move by the blow of [an object with] weight, since [otherwise] they will not move. The shapes of the atoms are ungraspably many, but not unlimited. For there are none which are hooked or trident-shaped or ring-shaped; for these shapes are easily broken and the atoms are impassible. They have their own shapes which can be contemplated by reason. The atom is so called not because it is the minimal [particle], but because it cannot be divided, since it is impassible and does not participate in void.

TEXT 78: Aetius 1.20.2 = *Dox.Gr.* p. 318 (271 U)

Epicurus [says that] void, place, and space differ [only] in name.

TEXT 79: Sextus *M* 8.329 (272 U)

... Epicurus, for example, thinks that he has offered the most power-ful demonstration that the void exists: "If motion exists, void exists; but motion does indeed exist; therefore void exists."

TEXT 80: Sextus *M* 10.2 (271 U—addendum)

Therefore, we must understand that according to Epicurus one part of the nature which is termed intangible is called 'void', one part 'place', and one part 'space'. The names vary according to different applications [of the intellect], since the nature which is designated 'void' when it is empty of every body is called 'place' when it is occupied by a body and becomes 'space' when bodies pass through it. In Epicurus, however, it is called by the general term 'intangible nature' because it is deprived of 'touch' in the sense of resistance.

TEXT 81: Sextus *M* 3.98 (273* U—addendum)

Then, as the Epicureans too say, the straight line in the void is indeed straight, but it does not turn because even the void itself is not receptive of motion either in whole or in part.

TEXT 82: Sextus *M* 10.257 (275 U)

... which Epicurus too agreed with when he said that body was con-ceived as an aggregate of shape and size and resistance and weight.

TEXT 83: Simplicius *Commentary on Aristotle's Physics* 232a23 ff. *CIAG* 10.938.17–22 (277 U)

For unless every magnitude were divisible, it would not always be pos-sible for a slower object to move a lesser distance in an equal time than a quicker one. For slower and quicker objects cover the atomic and indi-visible [distance] in the same time, since if [one] took more time, it would cover in the equal time a [distance] less than the indivisible [distance]. And that is why the Epicureans too think all [bodies] move at equal speed through indivisible [distances], so that they can avoid having their atomic [quantities] be divided and so no longer atomic.

TEXT 84: Aetius 1.12.5 = *Dox.Gr.* p. 311 (275, 280 U)

Epicurus [says that] the primary and simple bodies are ungraspable, and that the compounds formed from them all have weight. Atoms sometimes move in a straight line, sometimes in a swerve, and those which move upwards do so by collision and rebound.

TEXT 85: Aetius 1.23.4 = *Dox.Gr.* 319–320 (280 U)

Epicurus says there are two kinds of motion, the straight and the swerve.

TEXT 86: Plutarch *On the Generation of the Soul in the Timaeus* 1015bc (281 U)

... they do not concede to Epicurus that the atom can swerve the tiniest bit, on the grounds that he introduces a causeless motion coming from not being.

TEXT 87: Simplicius *Commentary on Aristotle's De Caelo* 275b29 *CIAG* 7.242.18–26(284 U)

For they [Leucippus, Democritus, and Epicurus] said that the principles were unlimited in number, and they also thought that they were atomic and indivisible and impassible, because they were dense and did not have a share of the void; for they said that division takes place where there is something void in bodies, and also that these atoms, being separated from each other in the unlimited void and differing in shape and size and position and ordering, move in the void and that they catch up with each other and collide and that some rebound to any chance place while others get entangled with each other, in accordance with the symmetry of their shapes and sizes and positions and orderings; and in this way it comes about that the origin of compounds is produced.

TEXT 88: Alexander of Aphrodisias *On Mixture* 214.28–215.8 (290 U)

Epicurus wanted to avoid what Democritus said followed for those who say that blending occurs by means of the juxtaposition of the components of the blend, and himself said that blending occurs by means of the juxtaposition of certain bodies, though not of bodies which are themselves mixed and [still] preserved in the division, (215) but rather of bodies that are broken down into elements and atoms from which each of [those bodies] is a sort of compound, one being wine, another water, another honey, another something else; and then he says that the blend occurs by a certain kind of reciprocal compounding of those bodies from which the components of the blend were constituted; and it is these which produce the blended body, not the water and the wine, but [it is] the atoms which make up the water, as one might call them, which are blended together with those which make up the wine by a destruction and generation of certain [bodies]. For the breakdown of each into its elements is a form of destruction, and the compounding produced from the elements themselves is ‹a sort of genesis›.

TEXT 89: Sextus *M* 10.219–227 (294 U)

219. According to the account of Demetrius of Laconia, Epicurus says that time is a property of properties which accompanies days and nights and hours and feelings and absences of feeling and motions and states of rest. For all of these are accidental properties of certain things, and since it accompanies all of these, time would not unreasonably be called a property of properties. **220.** For in general, to go back a bit in order to promote the comprehension of our argument, some existing things exist in their own right while others are observed to be dependent on things which exist in their own right. And the things which exist in their own right are things like substances (for example, body and void), while their so-called accidents are the things observed to be dependent on the things which exist in their own right. **221.** Of these accidents, some are inseparable from that of which they are the accidents, and some are of such a nature as to be separated. Those which are inseparable from that of which they are the accidents, then, are, for example, resistance [as an accident] of body and yielding [as an accident] of void. **222.** For a body cannot ever be thought of without resistance, nor can void be thought of without yielding; rather, resistance is a permanent accident of the one and yielding of the other. Those which are not inseparable from that of which they are the accidents are, for example, motion and rest. **223.** For compound bodies are neither in perpetual motion without opportunity for rest, nor are they perpetually in a state of not moving; rather, they sometimes have motion as an accident and sometimes rest. By contrast, the atom, when it is on its own, is in perpetual motion. For [while moving] it must either meet up with void or with a body; but if it meets with void, it moves through it because of its yielding, and if it meets with a body, its motion is a rebound away from it as a result of its resistance. **224.** These, then, are the properties which time accompanies, I mean day and night and hours and feelings and absences of feeling and motion and rest. For day and night are properties of the surrounding air, day occurring when the sun illuminates it and night coming along when it is deprived of the sun's light. **225.** An hour is a part of either a day or a night, and so again is a property of the air, just as day and night are. And time is co-extensive with every day and every night and hour, which is why night and day are said to be long or short, our reference being to the time which is an accident of [each of] these. And the feelings and absences of feeling are either [states of] pleasure or pain, which is why they are not substances but rather properties of those who have a pleasant or painful experience; but properties are not without [reference to] time. **226.** In addition, motion too and rest as well are, as we have already established, properties of bodies and are not separable from time. For we measure by time the speed or slowness of motion, and again the greater or lesser extent of a period of rest. **227.** But from all this it is evident that Epicurus thinks that time is an incorporeal, though not in the same sense as the Stoics do. For they, as we have said, posited that time is an incorporeal which is conceived of all by itself, while Epicurus thinks that it is an accident of certain things.

TEXT 90: Simplicius *Commentary on Aristotle's Physics* 203b15 *CIAG* 9.466, 31–467.4 (297 U)

There is a fourth point which is hard to stare down: the fact that everything which is limited seems to be limited by something. For if everything which is limited is limited by something which is external to itself, then that external thing by which it is limited is itself either unlimited or limited. And if it is unlimited, then we immediately have [the conclusion] that the unlimited exists. And if it is limited, for example, the earth, then this too is limited by something else, and so on without limit. And if it goes on without limit, the unlimited exists. For one will never get one's hands on the final limit, if indeed this too is limited by something else. The Epicureans, according to Alexander, relied on this argument above all else when they said that the totality was unlimited, because everything which is limited by something has outside it something which is [in turn] limited. And Aristotle mentions this as a quite old argument.

TEXT 91: Aetius 2.4.10 = *Dox.Gr.* p. 331 (305 U)

Epicurus [says that] the cosmos is destroyed in very many ways: for [it is destroyed] in the manner of an animal and in the manner of a plant and in lots of [other] ways.

TEXT 92: Aetius 1.4.1–4 = *Dox.Gr.* p. 289–291 (308* U)

1. So the cosmos was compounded and endowed with its rounded [lit.: bent] shape in the following manner.

Because the atomic bodies, which move without providence and in a random manner, were constantly moving at the greatest of speeds, many bodies were assembled together in the same place for this reason, and had a variety of shapes and sizes ⟨and weights⟩. 2. When they were assembling in the same place, the larger and heavier bodies, at all events, moved towards the bottom and settled; but the small, round, smooth, and slippery ones were pushed out in the concourse of atoms and so moved into the upper regions. So when the force of the blows [of atomic collisions] stopped raising them up and the blow[s] no longer carried them into the upper regions, but they were prevented from moving downwards, they were squeezed into the places which were able to receive them. And these were the places around about, and the majority of the bodies were bent around to these places. By becoming entangled with each other during the bending they generated the sky.

3. Retaining the same nature and being varied, as was said, the atoms which were pushed out to the upper regions produced the nature of the heavenly bodies. The majority of the bodies which were evaporated upwards struck the air and expelled it. And [the air], being made wind-like during its movement and gathering together the heavenly bodies, drove them around with itself and by this twisting produced their present circular movement in the upper regions.

And then the earth was produced from the [bodies] which settled [at the bottom], and from those which were raised upwards the sky, fire, and air [were produced]. 4. Since a great deal of matter was still contained in the earth and this was packed densely by the blows of the [atomic] bodies and by those from the rays of the heavenly bodies, [the earth's] entire configuration, which was made up of small particles, was squeezed together and [so] produced the nature of fluids. And since this [nature] was disposed to flow, it moved down into the hollow places and those able to receive it and contain it; that, or the water all by itself hollowed out the existing places by settling [there].

So the most important parts of the cosmos were produced in this way.

TEXT 93: Sextus *M* 7.267 (310 U)

Epicurus and his followers thought they were able to indicate the conception of man ostensively, saying: "man is this sort of form together with possession of life."

TEXT 94: Aetius 4.4.6 = *Dox.Gr.* p. 390 (312 U)

Democritus and Epicurus say the soul has two parts, one which is rational and is situated in the chest area, and the other which is non-rational and is spread throughout the entire compound of the body.

TEXT 95: Aetius 4.3.11 = *Dox.Gr.* p. 388–389 (315 U)

Epicurus [says that the soul is] a blend of four things, a certain kind of fiery stuff, a certain kind of airy stuff, a certain kind of breathlike stuff and a fourth something which is nameless. (This was the power of sense-perception for him.) Of these, the breath provides motion, the air rest, the hot the apparent heat of the body, and the nameless element the [power of] sense-perception in us. For sense-perception is in none of the named elements.

TEXT 96: Aetius 4.8.10 = *Dox.Gr.* p. 395 (317 U)

Leucippus, Democritus, and Epicurus [say that] sense-perception and thought occur when images approach from the outside. For we apply neither [sense-perception nor thought] to anything in the absence of an image striking from the outside.

TEXT 97: Aetius 4.13.1 = *Dox.Gr.* p. 403 (318 U)

Leucippus, Democritus, and Epicurus thought that the visual experience occurred by means of the reception of images.

TEXT 98: Alexander of Aphrodisias *Commentary on Aristotle's De Sensu* 438a5 ff. *CIAG* 3.1, 34.18–22 (319 U)

[Democritus] himself, and before him Leucippus and after him the Epicureans, think that certain images, which are of the same shape as the objects from which they flow, flow from them and strike the eyes of those who are seeing and that this is how seeing occurs. As a proof of this he offers the fact that there is always in the pupil of those who are seeing a reflection and image of what is seen, and this is exactly what the act of seeing is.

TEXT 99: Aetius 4.19.2 = *Dox.Gr.* p. 408 (321 U)

Epicurus [says that] the voice is a flow sent out from those who make utterances or produce sounds or noises. This flow is broken up into particles of the same shape. ("Of the same shape" means that the round are like the round and the angular and the triangular are like those of those types.) And when these strike the organs of hearing the perception of voice is produced.

TEXT 100: London Scholiast on Dionysius Thrax, *Grammatici Graeci* 1.3, p. 482.13–19 (Hilgard) (322 U)

Epicurus, Democritus, and the Stoics say that voice is a body. For everything which can act or be acted upon is a body. For example, iron: it is acted upon by fire and acts on men or wood. So if voice can act and be acted upon, it is a body. But it acts, since we proceed to enjoyment when we hear a voice or a lyre; and it is acted upon, as when we are speaking and the wind blows, which makes it harder to hear our voice.

TEXT 101: Censorinus *De Die Natali* 4.9 (333 U)

Democritus of Abdera first held that men were created from water and mud. And Epicurus' view is not much different: for he believed that when the mud became warm, first there grew wombs of some kind or another which clung to the earth by roots, and these sent forth infants and then provided a natural supply of milky fluid for them, under the guidance of nature. When these [infants] had been brought up in this manner and reached maturity, they then propagated the human race.

TEXT 102: Origen *Against Celsus* 1.24 (334 U)

As to this, one should also say that a deep and arcane debate about the nature of names emerged: are names conventional, as Aristotle thinks; or natural, as the Stoics believe (for the first utterances imitate the things the utterances are applied to, and accordingly they introduce [them] as elements of a kind for etymology); or are names natural, as Epicurus teaches—in a manner different from that of the Stoics, since the first men burst forth with certain sounds which were applied to things?

TEXT 103: Proclus *Commentary on Plato's Cratylus* 16, 17 (pp. 6 and 8–9 Boissonade, 335 U)

16. That Pythagoras and Epicurus shared the view of Cratylus, while Democritus and Aristotle shared that of Hermogenes.
17. That [names are] natural in four senses. For either [they are natural] as the substances of animals and plants are (both their parts and the wholes), or as their activities and powers are (for example, the lightness and heat of fire), or as shadows and reflections in mirrors are, or as crafted images which resemble their own archetypes are. Epicurus, then,

thought that names were natural in the first[34] sense, as being primary functions of nature: as the voice and vision and as seeing and hearing [are natural], in the same way naming [is natural]. So that names too are natural in the sense of functions of nature. But Cratylus [says that names are natural] in the second sense; that is why he says that each thing has its own proper name, since it was given specifically [to that thing] by the first name-givers in a craftsmanlike fashion based on an understanding [of that thing]. For Epicurus said that these men [the first name-givers] did not give names based on an understanding of things, but because they were moved in a natural fashion, like those who cough and sneeze and bellow and bark and lament.

TEXT 104: Aetius 4.7.4 = *Dox.Gr.* p. 393 (336 U)

Democritus and Epicurus [said that the soul] is mortal and perishes with the body.

TEXT 105: Sextus *M* 9.25 (353 U)

Epicurus thinks that men have derived the conception of god from presentations [received] while asleep. For, he says, since large anthropomorphic images strike them while they sleep they supposed that some such anthropomorphic gods also existed in reality.

TEXT 106: Aetius 1.7.34 = *Dox.Gr.* p. 306 (355 U)

Epicurus [says that] the gods are anthropomorphic and can be contemplated by reason as a result of the fineness of the nature of their images.

TEXT 107: Sextus *M* 9.178 (357 U)

And again, if [the divine] exists, it is either vocal or non-vocal. Well, to say that god is non-vocal is completely absurd and in conflict with the common conceptions. But if [the divine] is vocal, then it uses its voice and has speech organs, like lungs and windpipe and tongue and mouth. But this is absurd and almost as bad as the myths told by Epicurus.

---

34. Usener emends this to 'second'; but from the larger context it seems clear that Proclus rather sloppily groups the first two senses together as a new 'first sense', and is equally sloppy in his reference to Cratylus' use of the 'second' sense.

TEXT 108: Aetius 1.7.7 = *Dox.Gr.* p. 300 (361 U)

[An Epicurean speaks]: Both [Anaxagoras and Plato] share this error, because they portrayed god as being concerned for human affairs and as making the cosmos for the sake of man. For a blessed and indestructible animal, overflowing with good things and free of any share of what is bad, is completely preoccupied with the continuance of his own happiness and indestructibility and so is not concerned with human affairs. For he would be wretched, like a workman or builder, if he undertook burdens and felt concern for the creation of the cosmos.

TEXT 109: Lactantius *On the Anger of God* 13.20–22 (374 U)

20. And if this explanation [for the existence of bad things] . . . is true, then that argument of Epicurus is refuted. "God," he says, "either wants to eliminate bad things and cannot, or can but does not want to, or neither wishes to nor can, or both wants to and can. 21. If he wants to and cannot, then he is weak—and this does not apply to god. If he can but does not want to, then he is spiteful—which is equally foreign to god's nature. If he neither wants to nor can, he is both weak and spiteful and so not a god. If he wants to and can, which is the only thing fitting for a god, where then do bad things come from? Or why does he not eliminate them?" 22. I know that most of the philosophers who defend [divine] providence are commonly shaken by this argument and against their wills are almost driven to admit that god does not care, which is exactly what Epicurus is looking for.

TEXT 110: Aetius 1.29.5 = *Dox.Gr.* p. 326 (375 U)

Epicurus says that all things [occur] by necessity, by choice, and by chance.

TEXT 111: Simplicius *Commentary on Aristotle's Physics* 198b29 *CIAG* 9.371.30–372.16 (377* U)

In cases where everything happened as though it were for the sake of some goal, these [creatures] were preserved because, although they were formed by chance, they were formed as suitable compounds; but in other cases [the creatures] perished and still do perish, as Empedocles refers to "oxlike creatures with human faces". . . . The ancient natural philosophers who said that material necessity was the cause of things which come to be seem to hold this opinion, and among later thinkers so do the Epicureans. Their error comes, as Alexander says, from thinking that everything which comes to be for the sake of some goal comes to be by intention and calculation and from seeing that things which come about by nature do not come to be in this way. But this is not so.

TEXT 112: Plutarch *On Stoic Self-Contradictions* 1050bc (378 U)

(1050b) . . . And yet Epicurus somehow twists about and exercises his ingenuity **(1050c)** in contriving to free and liberate voluntary action from [the necessity of] eternal motion, in order not to leave vice immune to blame.

TEXT 113: Aetius 1.29.6 = *Dox.Gr.* p. 326 (380 U)

Epicurus [says that chance is] a cause which is unstable [or: uncertain] with respect to persons, times, and places.

TEXT 114: Maximus the Abbott *Gnomologium* 14 (388 U)

If god acted in accordance with the prayers of men, all men would rather quickly be destroyed, since they constantly pray for many sufferings to befall each other.

Ethics

TEXT 115: Plutarch *Against Colotes* 1127a (8 U)

And when they write, they write about politics to discourage us from practicing politics, and write about rhetoric to discourage us from practicing rhetoric, and about kingship to discourage us from consorting with kings.

TEXT 116: Ammianus Marcellinus 30.4.3 (51 U)

The rich genius of Plato defines this calling, i.e., forensic oratory, as an image of a part of politics; but Epicurus calls it "a vile technique." . . .

TEXT 117: Seneca *Letters on Ethics* 8.7 (199 U)

"You ought to be a slave to philosophy in order to achieve true liberty."

TEXT 118: Porphyry *To Marcella* 30 (200 U)

"When the flesh cries out, be assured that the [answering] cry of the soul can be explained by natural science. The cry of the flesh: not to be hungry, not to be thirsty, not to be cold. And while it is difficult for the soul to prevent these things, it is dangerous to neglect nature which daily proclaims self-sufficiency to the soul via the [flesh] which is intimately bonded to it."

TEXT 119: Porphyry *To Marcella* 27 (202✩ U)

"So he who follows nature and not groundless opinions is in all things self-sufficient. For every possession is wealth when it comes to satisfying nature, while even the greatest wealth is poverty when it comes to the unlimited desires."

TEXT 120: Porphyry *To Marcella* 29 (203 U)

"Insofar as you are stymied, you are stymied because you forget nature; for you burden yourself with unlimited fears and desires."

TEXT 121: Plutarch *A Pleasant Life* 1105e (213 U)

"Sweet is the memory of a dead friend."

TEXT 122: Maximus the Abbot *Gnomologium* 8 (214 U, 199 A)

"Do not avoid doing trivial favours, for you will seem to be like this in important matters too."

TEXT 123: Maximus the Abbot *Gnomologium* 66 (215 U, 200 A)

"Do not turn away the request of an enemy in need; just protect yourself, for he is no better than a dog."

TEXT 124: Porphyry *To Marcella* 31 (221 U)

"Empty is the argument of the philosopher by which no human disease is healed; for just as there is no benefit in medicine if it does not drive out bodily diseases, so there is no benefit in philosophy if it does not drive out the disease of the soul."

TEXT 125: Plutarch *Against Colotes* 1117f (222 U)

One of Epicurus' doctrines is that no one except the wise man is unshakeably persuaded of anything.

TEXT 126: Vatican Scholiast on Dionysius Thrax, *Grammatici Graeci* 1.3, p. 108.27–29 (Hilgard) (227b U)

This is how the Epicureans define craft: a craft is a method which effects what is advantageous for [human] life. "Effects" is used in the sense of "produces."

TEXT 127: Plutarch *A Pleasant Life* 1093c (229a U)

They even reject the pleasures which come from mathematics!

TEXT 128: Sextus *PH* 3.194 (398 U)

Hence, the Epicureans too think that they are proving that pleasure is naturally worth choosing; for they say that animals, as soon as they are born and while they are still uncorrupted, have an impulse to pleasure and avoid pains.

TEXT 129: Alexander of Aphrodisias *De Anima CIAG* Supp. 2.1, p. 150.33–34 (398 U)

The Epicureans held that what is first congenial to us, unqualifiedly, is pleasure, but they say that as we get older this pleasure becomes articulated.

TEXT 130: Athenaeus *Deipnosophists* 12, 546f (409 U)

And Epicurus says, "the principle and root of all good is the pleasure of the belly; and the sophisticated and refined [goods] are referred to this one."

TEXT 131: Plutarch *Against Colotes* 1122e (411 U)

All by themselves and without a teacher, these noble and smooth and agreeable motions of the flesh beckon, as they themselves say, even men who refuse to admit that they are swayed and softened by them.

TEXT 132: Plutarch *A Pleasant Life* 1090b (413 U)

So if the soul supposes that its good lies in the stable condition of the body and in confidence about [the condition of] the body [as Epicurus thinks it does], then it cannot live out its life free of fear and upset. For the body is not only subject to storms and squalls from outside itself, like the sea, but from within itself it generates more and greater upsets.

TEXT 133: Damascius *Lectures on the Philebus*, 190 (p. 91 Westerink; 416 U)

Even Epicurus, referring to natural pleasure, says that it is katastematic.

TEXT 134: Plutarch *A Pleasant Life* 1088c–e (417 U)

(1088c) ... Epicurus has assigned a common limit to [the pleasures], the removal of all that causes pain, as though nature increased pleasure up to the point where it eliminates the painful, but did not permit it to make any further increase in its size, though it admits of certain non-necessary variations once it gets free of distress. The journey [which we make] towards this goal, in the company of desire, constitutes the [full] measure of pleasure and it is certainly short and economical. **(1088d)** That is why when they sense their stinginess in this area, they transfer their goal from the body, which is a barren field, to the soul, in order to acquire there pastures and meadows lushly overflowing with pleasures . . .

So don't you think that these men do well, in starting from the body, which is the first place where pleasure makes its appearance, and going on to the soul as something more secure which perfects everything within itself? . . .

(1088e) . . . but if you hear them crying out and shouting that the soul by nature finds joy and tranquillity in no existing thing except the pleasures of the body, whether present or anticipated, and that this is its good, don't you think that they are using the soul as a kind of decanter for the body and that they suppose that by pouring pleasure, like wine, from a broken-down and leaky container to this [new container] and aging it [there] they are doing something more impressive and valuable?

TEXT 135: Stobaeus *Anthology* 3.17.34 (vol. 3 p. 501 W-H; 422 U)

"We need pleasure when we are in pain because of its absence; but when we are not in this condition, and are in a stable state of sense-perception, then there is no need for pleasure. For it is not the needs of nature which produce injustice from without, but the desire based on groundless opinions."

TEXT 136: Plutarch *A Pleasant Life* 1091b (423 U)

He says, "for unsurpassable joy is produced by comparison with a great bad thing which one has escaped; and this is the nature of the good, if one applies [one's intellect] properly and then takes a firm stand, but does not stroll around babbling emptily about the good."

TEXT 137: Plutarch *A Pleasant Life* 1099d (436 U)

As they say, remembering previous goods is the most important factor contributing to a pleasant life.

TEXT 138: Aristocles, quoted by Eusebius at *Prep. Ev.* 14.21.3 (442 U)

It is better to endure these particular pains, so that we might experience greater pleasures; and it is advantageous to refrain from these particular pleasures so that we might not suffer from more burdensome pains.

TEXT 139: Porphyry *On Abstinence* 1.51 (463 U)

Variations in one's nourishment cannot possibly dissolve the disturbances of the soul, and indeed cannot even increase the pleasure in the
flesh; for this too reaches its limit as soon as the removal of pain is
achieved.

TEXT 140: Stobaeus *Anthology* 3.17.22 (vol. 3 p. 495 W-H; 469 U)

"I am grateful to blessed Nature, because she made what is necessary
easy to acquire and what is hard to acquire unnecessary."

TEXT 141: Porphyry *To Marcella* 27 (471 U)

"It is rare to find a man who is ‹poor› with regard to the goal set by
nature and rich with regard to groundless opinions. For no imprudent
man is satisfied by what he has, but rather is distressed by what he does
not have. So just as people with a fever are always thirsty and desire the
most inconsistent things because of the malignancy of their ‹disease›, so
too those whose souls are in a bad condition always feel that they are
totally impoverished and enmeshed in all sorts of desires as a result of
their gluttony."

TEXT 142: Aelian *Miscellaneous History* 4.13 (473 U)

"He for whom a little is not sufficient finds nothing sufficient."

TEXT 143: Porphyry *To Marcella* 28 (476 U)

"Self-sufficiency is the greatest wealth of all."

TEXT 144: Porphyry *To Marcella* 28 (478 U)

"Most men are afraid of parsimony in their life-style and because of
this fear proceed to actions which are most likely to produce it."

TEXT 145: Porphyry *To Marcella* 28 (479 U)

"Many men attain wealth but do not find therein an escape from their
problems; rather, they exchange them for greater problems."

TEXT 146: Porphyry *To Marcella* 29 (480 U)

"By hard labour fit for a beast a great quantity of wealth is heaped up;
but life is made miserable."

TEXT 147: Porphyry *To Marcella* 29 (485 U)

"For a man is unhappy either because of fear or because of unlimited and groundless desire; and by reining these in he can produce for himself the reasoning [which leads to] blessedness."

TEXT 148: Seneca *Letters on Ethics* 12.10 (487 U)

"It is bad to live with necessity, but there is no necessity to live with necessity."

TEXT 149: Plutarch *On Peace of Mind* 474c (490 U)

"He who has least need of tomorrow will approach it with the greatest pleasure."

TEXT 150: Seneca *Letters on Ethics* 24.22–23 (496–498 U)

Epicurus reproaches those who long for death no less than those who fear it, and says: "it is absurd to pursue death because you are weary of life, when you have made death worth pursuing by your way of life." In another place he says something similar: "So great is the folly, nay madness, of men that some are driven to death by the fear of death." . . . "What is so absurd as to seek death when you have made your own life troubled by fearing death."

TEXT 151: Athenaeus *Deipnosophists* 12, 547a (512 U)

"I spit upon the honourable and on those who vainly admire it, whenever it produces no pleasure."

TEXT 152: Clement of Alexandria *Stromates* 6.2,24.10 p. 441 Stählin (519 U)

"The greatest fruit of justice is freedom from disturbance."

TEXT 153: Arrian, *Discourses of Epictetus* 2.20.6–7 (523 U)

6. So too Epicurus, when he wishes to abolish the natural community of men with one another, makes use of the very thing he is destroying. **7.** For what does he say? Don't be deceived, men, or misled or mistaken: there is no natural community of rational beings with each other. Believe me: those who say otherwise are deceiving you and reasoning falsely.

TEXT 154: Stobaeus *Anthology* 4.143 (vol. 4 p. 90 W-H; 530 U)

"The laws exist for the sake of the wise, not so that they will not commit injustice but so that they will not suffer injustice."

TEXT 155: Plutarch *A Pleasant Life* 1090cd (532 U)

(1090c) . . . for they say that those who break the law and commit injustice live in fear and misery for all time, because even if they can escape detection, it is nevertheless impossible to be confident about escaping detection. **(1090d)** That is the source of the fear about the future which always weighs on them and does not permit them to rejoice or be of good cheer about the present.

TEXT 156: Plutarch *A Pleasant Life* 1104b (534 U)

For Epicurus does not think that one ought to restrain [people] from injustice by any means other than the fear of punishment.

TEXT 157: Plutarch *A Pleasant Life* 1097a (544 U)

And they themselves say that benefitting [others] is pleasanter than receiving benefits.

TEXT 158: Plutarch *On How to Listen to Poets* 37a (548 U)

"It is not great sums of money or a mass of possessions, nor even certain political offices and powers, which produce happiness and blessedness, but rather freedom from pain and gentleness in our feelings and a disposition of soul which measures out what is natural."

TEXT 159: Aelian *Miscellaneous Histories* 4.13 (602 U)

[Epicurus] said that he was ready to rival Zeus for happiness, as long as he had a barley cake and some water.

Index

The first number of each citation refers to the text number; numbers after the period are the references within each text.